ACROSS THE PIAVE

A Personal Account of
the British Forces in Italy
1917-1919

Norman Gladden

SAPERE
BOOKS

ACROSS THE PIAVE

Published by Sapere Books.
24 Trafalgar Road, Ilkley, LS29 8HH
United Kingdom

saperebooks.com

ISBN: 978-1-80055-705-5.

TABLE OF CONTENTS

PREFACE

The Italian Front was, in terms of the number of British troops involved, the smallest of the 'side shows' in the First World War. It was also, of all the theatres of war, the one where the British soldier stood the greatest chance of survival. No fewer than five out of every nine men sent to the Western Front were killed or wounded. In Italy the casualty rate was only one in twenty-one.

Norman Gladden served in Italy with the 11th Battalion, Northumberland Fusiliers, from November 1917 until the end of the war, having previously seen action on the Somme and at Passchendaele. As he explains in *Across the Piave*, Italy, with its snow-capped mountains and its ancient cities, seemed a paradise after the rain and mud and desolation of Flanders. The welcome which the British troops received as they marched through Italy on their way to the line recalled the enthusiastic scenes in Northern France in the heady days of August 1914. Conditions, both in and out of the trenches, were infinitely better than those on the Western Front. The Austrians, though some of their divisions were of high quality, were not such formidable opponents as the Germans: they were less aggressive, more inclined to live and let live. The Austrian air force was timid and unenterprising, and the sleep of troops in the rest areas was seldom disturbed by enemy bombing. At times the Italian Front was so quiet that it was difficult to believe there was a war on.

When the first British and French contingents arrived in Italy, the Italians had partially recovered from the crushing defeat inflicted on them at Caporetto, and had succeeded in halting the advance of the victorious Austro-German forces on the Grappa-Piave line. The Piave, whose swirling waters figure prominently in Dr Gladden's narrative, became the symbol of Italian resistance. By the end of 1917 it was clear that the Austrian attempt to break into Italy had failed. The Germans withdrew their divisions, and for the next nine months the trench line remained more or less stationery. In June 1918 the Austrians launched a major offensive in a desperate bid to knock Italy out of the war. They were driven back after fierce fighting, in which Dr Gladden's battalion played a notable part. In his vivid account of the battle, Dr Gladden observes that this was the first occasion in two years of warfare on which he actually saw and fired at the enemy. The 11th Northumberland Fusiliers also distinguished themselves in the forcing of the Piave by Lord Cavan's Tenth Army in October 1918, the first and most important phase in a series of operations which were to culminate in the victory of Vittorio Veneto and the complete collapse of Austria-Hungary.

For those who may be unfamiliar with the course of the Italian campaign, Dr Gladden has prefaced each main section of his book with a short historical introduction.

Christopher Dowling
Imperial War Museum

INTRODUCTION

This narrative of my experiences with the Italian Expeditionary Force during the First World War originated in a series of diary notes which I managed to maintain from the day I crossed to France on 30 August 1916, to participate in the dreary closing stages of the First Battle of the Somme, which had been tragically launched on 1 July, until I returned home from Italy on 1 February 1919, as described herein.

During the years immediately following the war the original diary was lengthened into a more detailed version on similar lines. Subsequently it was reshaped in narrative form as a full account, under the title *Full Pack*, of what happened to one young Tommy during those desperate years. The middle section was published by William Kimber under the title *Ypres, 1917*, in 1967, marking the 50th anniversary of the Battles of Messines, Third Ypres and Passchendaele, which I was fortunate both to suffer and to survive. The present text follows on the former work, covering the time I spent in Italy. The early phase about the Somme, a more awful and frustrating experience than either of the two so far published, remains in typescript.

As a permanent civil servant it would not have been easy to misrepresent my age — not that I wanted to — for while I was intensely patriotic and had no intention whatever of 'dodging the column', as we called it, I was not deluded by the romantic visions of the heroic nature of war that swept across Europe at the outbreak. From the very beginning, the pictures in the many war journals that flooded from the press, and the reports from the front, were there to understand had one wished.

Towards the end of 1915 I attested, and took the King's shilling under the Derby scheme, the State's last attempt to meet the war's manpower needs without conscription. It could well have been successful had our leadership been more enlightened, for the early recruitment had been tremendous and a great credit to Britain and the Empire.

I was recalled to the colours, as the scheme provided, the following May, just three months before the then official enlistment age of 19; and served with the 2/1 Hertfordshires at Hertford, Newmarket and Harrogate. With the speeding up of drafting following the great Somme losses, my training was compressed to an impossibly short four months and I went abroad with my battalion's second draft, to join the 7th Northumberland Fusiliers in the 50th Division on the Somme, where, by the end of the year, I had been converted into an old sweat, taken part in the battles for Le Sars and the Butte de Warlencourt, seen my dearest pal fatally wounded, contracted trench feet through constant immersion and returned a casualty to Blighty, via No 6 General Hospital at Rouen, where I arrived on Christmas morning. After kind treatment by the military hospital services and people of Cardiff and Bridgend, and much less sympathetic re-training at the regiment's depot at Catterick, I returned to France on 5 May 1917 to join the 11th Northumberland Fusiliers in the 23rd Division, with which I served with only one home leave, and that after the armistice, until my discharge early in 1919.

There is nothing heroic or exceptional about my story. I had a strong sense of duty, which the present generation will find difficult to understand. What happened to me happened to millions of others, too many of whom were less fortunate. My run of luck — if that is the right word — was quite phenomenal. The experience, which I have set down as honestly as I can, has had the inestimable virtue of reducing life's subsequent and inevitable disappointments to size, and has made me realise how good it is to be alive.

Norman Gladden

HISTORICAL NOTE: ITALY AT WAR, 1915-1917

When the Great War broke out in the first days of August 1914, Italy belonged to a Triple Alliance with Germany and Austria-Hungary which dated back to 1882, but Austria-Hungary was still the traditional enemy, against whom she had territorial claims. It was no surprise therefore when, on 3 August, Italy declared her neutrality in the emerging struggle. Her official objective was to secure those Italian-speaking areas on her northern frontiers in the Trentino and Istria which she had failed to obtain in 1866 as part of her reward for supporting Germany in her brief war with Austria, when the latter had been compelled to transfer to Italy a large part of Venetia. The Italian people undoubtedly favoured the Western Allies but their government at first hoped to be able to extract acceptable terms from Austria-Hungary, who had plenty of other troubles on her hands. When these negotiations broke down, Italy was able to obtain firm promises from the Allies, which led to her declaration of war upon Austria-Hungary on 23 May 1915. Her break with Germany was deferred until 27 August 1916.

From the summer of 1915 to the autumn of 1917 the Italians undertook a series of fierce campaigns against the Austrian positions in the Trentino and on the Isonzo river, but, despite the great bravery of the Italian troops and the capture of a number of important positions, the Austrian defence was conducted with skill and determination; and the mountainous terrain made all fighting so costly that the losses to both sides were unusually high and out of all proportion to the advantages gained.

The Russian Revolution and the collapse of the Eastern Front in 1917 made it possible for the Austrians to deploy larger forces against the Italians and for the Germans to send General Otto von Below with the Fourteenth Army to Austria-Hungary's assistance. On 24 October 1917 a well-planned thrust by von Below's forces at a point just south of Caporetto on the right flank of the Italian positions on the Isonzo took the Italians completely by surprise. Within a couple of days the entire right of the Italian line was in hectic retreat to the Tagliamento river. Italy's call for aid could hardly be ignored by the Western Allies, however distasteful it might be to their military commands to release troops from the Western Front, which had so recently been subjected to unheard of strains. By 26 October the French had arranged to send their first two divisions and the War Cabinet in London had telegraphed Sir Douglas Haig, British commander-in-chief in France, to dispatch two divisions, the honour falling to the 23rd and the 41st Divisions. The new Italian Expeditionary Force, which was supported by two squadrons of the Royal Air Force, was placed under the command of General Sir Herbert Plumer (later Lord Plumer of Messines). It should be added that batteries of British heavy artillery were already supporting the Italians and some had been involved in the retreat, an incident vividly described by a distinguished eye-witness, the late Hugh Dalton, in his With the British Guns in Italy.

It was planned to send six British divisions. In addition to the 23rd and 41st already mentioned, the 5th, 7th, 21st and 48th were also assigned, but the dispatch of the 21st was cancelled.

As British and French troops streamed across the Alps by road and rail, the Italian armies, after further withdrawals, were establishing themselves along the right bank of the broad Piave river, leaving a large slice of the fertile Lombardian plain in Austrian hands. Beset by tremendous supply problems, the Austro-German drive had for the time being lost momentum. The great Caporetto offensive was officially closed by the enemy on 2 December 1917 and the Germans, eager for the return of their shock troops to the Western Front, ordered part of their reinforcements back to Germany, leaving the Austrians with a task that was to prove beyond their capacity. Yet for the time being the Italian high command, although thoroughly reconstructed, was still far from confident that there were sufficient resources to meet another enemy offensive. The Allied armies had to be prepared for every possible eventuality.

1: NEW ADVENTURE

The time was the first week of November, in the year 1917; the place, pleasant rural billets in the St Martin-au-Laert suburb of St Omer in northern France. We — members of 'B' Company, 11th Battalion Northumberland Fusiliers in the 23rd (Northern) Division — were rapidly recovering from our recent testing experience at Ypres and Passchendaele. For some days the billet had been filled with rumours that the division was about to move to another front; some said not to another part of the Western Front, but to places at the very ends of the earth. All the notorious spots of the world-flung battle line had been mentioned, from Salonika to Burma, not excluding Italy, which had been much in the news since the recent disaster at Caporetto. Yet we had placed little store upon this particular forecast, which seemed rather off the normal course for British military action. This was just our ignorance, for we were not then aware that British guns of the Royal Garrison Artillery had been supporting the Italians for some months past.

It need hardly be said that we were excited at the prospect of some degree of adventure invading our personal war, even though similar wild rumours in the past had raised our expectations only to be proved false. Yet with unmistakeable signs of an imminent move building up from day to day, we were not surprised when orders were issued for us to be ready to leave billets at 7 pm on 7 November, and we found ourselves really en route for 'oonoesware'. With the rest of the Lewis gun team, I had been detailed to join an advance party at the railhead to ensure that our equipment was properly stowed and readily available in case of emergency. Moreover, it was by no means unknown for quite large items of equipment to be mislaid, or even lost, on such occasions. Our task completed, we rejoined the rest of the company in freight trucks, and, packed thirty to a truck, at 1.30 am on 8 November 1917, our leisurely journey began.

We were still in the dark as to our destination. A last-minute rumour that we were to create a diversion in Albania sounded as reasonable as any, but I do not think we should have been very surprised to find ourselves converging upon another sector of the Western Front. For the moment, at least, we were in unusually high spirits. A new interest was entering our drab lives. Our morale was being boosted. This feeling was heightened by the accumulating evidence, as the day unfolded, that this was not just one of those routine jaunts to which we had become accustomed.

During the first morning we crossed the old battlefields of Arras and the Somme, along a brand new railway track which the army had relaid, passing through such memory-provoking places as the Achiets and battered Albert, with its inclining Madonna still held in position above the shattered town below. From the train we could see members of the Indian Labour Corps making things ship-shape again. All the garbage of war was being collected in heaps — stacks of rusty barbed wire and pickets, dumps of dud shells, shattered gun carriages and the like, all accumulating by the railside. Grass already covered the gaping shell-holes, weeds and moss were masking deserted dugouts. At a distance Albert itself, of such anguished memory, seemed little changed, battered and forlorn as it was, with its protecting guns now at work far beyond the distant ridges out of our hearing. This brief panoramic vision of the past was both disconcerting and difficult to accept. The hell of the

Somme, so recently corroborated by the somewhat different hell of Ypres, would remain much more real to me — and no doubt to my companions — than the tidied cemetery we had just passed. As I mused thus upon the hardly believable evidence of my eyes, the train continued to move parallel to the battle line. Eventually it ambled into Amiens, there to stop awhile and enable us to remove the cobwebs of the night.

During that evening we passed through the crowded suburbs of Paris, and I was excited to have my first glimpse of the Eiffel Tour, whose profile was just discernible in the falling dusk. Our leisurely gait continued: early the next morning we passed through Troyes, and Dijon during the afternoon. We were leaving the Western Front well behind us and a new expectancy seemed to invest the slowly-moving train. To our northern eyes the countryside, despite its autumn tinge, was becoming luxuriant and strange. At every halt — and in the very nature of our journeying these were frequent — we got down to stretch our legs, some to hurry along to the engine to draw boiling water for tea-making, at which we were expert.

It was on 10 November that our destination was at last confirmed. During the night we had passed through the large rail centre of Lyons and in the morning, as we moved steadily southwards, the bright beauty of the Rhone Valley gradually unfolded before our eyes. I gazed with a new delight upon the wonderful old town of Avignon, with its upstanding walls and the impressive bastion of the Palace of the Popes towering above the clustering houses. Already our progress was becoming something of a triumphal procession, for all along the line, at every inhabited place, the local people welcomed us enthusiastically. We were being made to feel that we belonged to a nation that was honoured in the world.

During the morning we reached Marseilles. Over the rooftops, in the setting of green-clad hills and wide-spreading harbour, I saw for the first time the intensely blue Mediterranean, and was filled with wonder at my good fortune. For a short while, as the train halted and our officers began to alight uncertainly from their first-class carriages, we thought that even now we might be switched to other transport. Marseilles, as we well knew, was one of the great communications centres of the war, a junction through which Allied troops passed to the very ends of the earth, for the Mediterranean was a comparatively safe sea for the transport of Allied troops and the war powerfully encompassed its eastern shores.

That evening the train, travelling eastwards, reached Toulon and we knew that Italy was our destination. When we opened the door of our truck on the morning of 11 November the train had halted at a station alongside a tall white flagstaff, from which floated a strange banner in red, white and green with a central shield — the ensign of Italy. We were at Ventimiglia, the first station across the frontier. I was sorry to have missed the French Riviera, which we had traversed during the night, but experienced a naive delight at having thus come to this romantic and beautiful land, a land with which I was to fall immediately in love and to revisit again and again in later years.

We were fortunate in the hour of our entry, for the autumn sun shone down upon that lovely coast with a clarity that caused everything to sparkle in its limpid light, and only at the meeting point between sea and sky did there seem to be any gradation between the two shades of blue. The railway line, an ugly mechanical despoiler of the lovely shore, curled in and out, now on rocky slopes poised precariously above the sea, now threading numerous tunnels through the hillside. We passed richly wooded valleys, with occasional glimpses of the peaks of the Maritime Alps towering beyond, and vineyards and orchards filled with vines and fig and palm and many subtropical plants, which were new to me. Waters of intense blueness were breaking in lazy white surf along the red-hued rocks, upon which square colour-washed houses firmly stood, their walls often painted with designs that gave a fairy touch to the scene.

Our reception by the dwellers in this demi-paradise was remarkably enthusiastic. We were going to our new war as to a triumph that traditionally came after the victory. Every building was decorated with bunting or Allied flags, and sometimes, unwittingly, with colours that may have belonged to the enemy, for they were not all easily identifiable. Every window was crammed with cheering humanity, some climbing even to the roof to welcome us. The peasants in vineyard and field stopped working as we passed to wave to us with their peculiar beckoning gesture, which we were soon copying with great amusement. At the stations we were amazed at the variety of multi-coloured uniforms worn by the officials, and were open-eyed at the Carabinieri — the soldier-policemen with short-slung rifles and Napoleonic hats — who invariably patrolled in pairs. It was immediately clear that the beauty of the Italian girls was no myth, and the distant kiss-throwing was enthusiastically reciprocated along the gaping sides of the train. At the halts they brought fruit and flowers, cigarettes and postcard views of the little towns, while that forward minority to whom the opposite sex is always an irresistible magnet massed forward at the door to receive these gifts from olive-complexioned goddesses, leaving the less demonstrative majority to draw back shyly but with feelings of no less delight.

The dirty old cattle trucks, loaded with uncouth males from the cold damp north, were garlanded with waving fronds of palm. If we were not really heroes, we were at that moment fully prepared to be heroic on behalf of such generous hosts, and it is now pleasant to remember that they were not to be disappointed in our performance.

During the morning we passed through San Remo, an international holiday resort much frequented before the war by the well-to-do, and came to Savona, a small commercial port sandwiched between the mountains and the sea. As the people of the town wished to see us, we were immediately ordered to make a ceremonial march through the main thoroughfares. We cleaned ourselves up as best we could, but our resources were quite inadequate for such an occasion, and we paraded with much grumbling, which was partly attributable to our general dislike at being made a show of. We were glad when the whole business was over. Perhaps this attitude, if understandable, was a little ungrateful.

As we marched through this quaint old place, down to the harbour and back, the streets were thronged with cheering crowds of drably-garbed townsfolk and brightly-uniformed officials. For the first time I saw the arcaded sidewalks and piazzas so typical of Italian towns, and I wondered at the time whether this fashion would not have been even more useful for keeping out of our rain than for avoiding the southern sunshine, not then realising how welcome the shade can be in the hot summers of Italy. Those covered sidewalks are all that I clearly remember of Savona, apart from the kindness of the townsfolk.

But our entry into Italy had not been without its tragedy. During the previous night one of our company officers had fallen from the train to his death. We knew that there had been 'celebrations' in the officers' carriages, but the whole business had been hushed up and we never knew the true facts. Stricter instructions were issued against climbing about outside the trucks when the train was in motion, no doubt to appease the official conscience; while yet another announcement of 'killed in action' tactfully avoided conveying to the bereaved relations what had really happened. We were critical of our masters and not very sorry for the victim. He had lost little time in making himself thoroughly unpopular as a snappy supercilious type, self-dedicated to keeping the rest of us in our proper places.

We moved out of Savona late in the afternoon, reaching Genoa in the evening, where a massive electric engine was attached to haul us over the mountains. In the siding there we talked with a group of Italian cadets, who were fluent in French, Isaac Doniger acting as general interpreter. They told us of Italy's great joy on learning that the Allies were sending aid, and of their great concern at the disaster at the front, which had certainly not been exaggerated. The cadets were very interested in our equipment, which we were naturally only too pleased to explain to them, and in the process we had our first lesson in Italian, practising such words as *si* for 'yes' and *pane*, pronounced 'pa-nay', for 'bread', basic expressions for a soldier to learn in any land.

The next morning the mountains had been left far behind, and we were crossing the Plains of Lombardy, the flattest land I had ever seen, now masked in ground-mist. The station platforms at Modena were crowded with peasant refugees with their sadly-meagre worldly goods, our first tangible evidence of this different war. Our long railway journey ended when we detrained at Mantovano, a small place beyond Mantova, the historic city better known to us as Mantua. The battalion marched back towards the city along a flat road, bordered on our right by vineyards and on our left by the waters of a wide lagoon. Crossing an ancient bridge, we were again welcomed enthusiastically by the dark-complexioned, black-garbed townsfolk, and for the first time in my life I caught a brief thrilling glimpse of the striking medieval architecture of Italy. School-day readings of Shakespeare and Scott were suddenly endowed with a verisimilitude they had never had before. This romantic historic land really existed! An interesting fact, that I noticed at the time, was the occasional inscription on the bridge and other municipal walls, which, despite the language barrier, clearly referred to the Republic of Venice. The notices did not seem very old and I was not able to understand their import. I knew vaguely that there had been a great Venetian Republic, recollecting of course *The Merchant of Venice*, and now I concluded that Mantua had once been part of it, though I did not then know that the city had only come back to the new Italy in 1866, some fifty years before.

We marched out of the town a few kilometres to the little hamlet of Grazie, and were there billeted in a large four-square country house, standing in its own grounds. The rooms were large and bare, with stone floors and plain plastered walls, unfurnished certainly, but one could hardly imagine much comfort even with furnishings. Everything was so cold out of the sunshine. This of course was what was intended, though it was to be some time before I came to realise it. As billets, however, the house left little room for grumbling, for it was far above the standards we had been used to in Flanders. We were not long in arranging our kits round the walls in regulation fashion and making ourselves at home.

Behind the scenes plans were well in hand to meet the grave eventualities for which our move had been decreed. The authorities, reacting as a matter of course, set to work to restore normal army routines with the least possible delay and, despite the obstacles in the way, it is surprising how effectively this was done.

On the morning of 13 November I experienced one of those personally uncomfortable moments of little real importance which, nevertheless, stood out above the normal monotony of our daily life in the ranks. Some registered mail had been stolen from our train and, to satisfy the Italian authorities, the order had gone forth that we should all be searched. Our officers were not pleased with this unwelcome duty, while we were angry at this further erosion of the last shreds of personal liberty. But I thought immediately, not of principles, but of my diary, which I had continued to keep against regulations. Such information as I noted down (though I was careful to omit any reference to persons and places) could conceivably have been of use to the enemy. I had visions of a firing squad or, at least, some dire punishment, and lest this should appear rather exaggerated at this distance of time, it should be realised that to us, habituated to the arbitrary ways of army discipline, anything was possible. Our billets were first thoroughly examined and then we were marched out on to the one-time lawn in front of the house to be searched. The officer came slowly along the ranks, looking at the contents of each man's pockets. As it happened the man immediately before me was a Polish Jew from the East End of London, a saturnine, unprepossessing individual, but one whose taciturnity and selfishness had earned him universal unpopularity. He was always flush with money, which he cared for with a meanness that had provoked general comment. In return, the company's intolerant attitude to him embodied all the historic reactions of the Christian to members of his race. On this occasion he displayed, with vehement protests, a pocket-book choked with notes, and he was so affronted that he made no effort to hide his great indignation from the officer, whom in fact he had no difficulty in satisfying.

We were for once unanimously on his side. Indeed he served to canalise and concentrate the indignation of us all. I was myself surprised that he was not run in for insolence on the spot. Clearly the officer himself was too tensed up by the situation to take note of particular incidents and for once the sergeant-major's voice was not raised to draw his attention to his normal responsibilities. As it was, the incident turned out to my advantage, for the officer, still obviously upset by the unexpected altercation, looked at the contents of my pockets, which I displayed apprehensively in my hands — the usual collection of objects that soldiers accumulate: pieces of string, a jack-knife, spare shoulder-badges, other odds and ends — and selecting my diary, quietly fanned its pages. I breathed with difficulty. He handed it back without comment, and the ordeal was over. No one present could have realised the conscience-stricken cowardice from which I had been relieved. The parade was shortly dismissed, nothing, of course, having been discovered.

We were quickly settling down in our new environment. It happened that Number 6 Platoon was billeted in an upstairs room. From a large window over the staircase there was an extensive view across the flat countryside northwards to a faint line of snow-capped mountain peaks, that sparkled in the bright morning sun. This was my first distant glimpse of the Alps and I was thrilled at the sight, which I stopped frequently to admire.

In the nearby farms we discovered an inexhaustible supply of small pipless grapes, which tasted like wine and cost next to nothing. I had my service-cap filled for half a lire (then the equivalent of threepence). But it was bread that we wanted. On our first afternoon, Rampton, a private in the company, with whom I had a nodding acquaintance, proposed a forage in the village for *pane*, the staff of life. The rest were already assiduously acquiring the post-prandial habit of siesta, and so we had the place to ourselves. The problem was to find a baker, but the few village shops had little to show. We saw some jolly little dark-eyed, olive-complexioned children playing in the square in front of the church, and, having overcome their initial terror for such fearsome strangers by making them gifts of ten *centissimi* pieces, we persuaded them to take us to the door of the *panificio*, where our immediate wants were satisfied. Further successful expeditions of this sort were almost immediately prevented by authority, for that very evening an order was issued putting the village and all 'estaminets', as we still called them, out of bounds. We took a poor view of this, not realising what big problems of supply the advent of such a large and hungry army could thrust upon local authorities already overwhelmed by war-time complications.

Always of a retiring disposition, I was at this period something of a lone wolf. Having lost in succession three dear companions in battle since my arrival in France in the late summer of 1916, I was resolved not to get too closely involved with anyone in future, lest I should become a sort of Job to him. On the other hand it was natural for us to hunt in pairs and I reserved myself the right to join up with another lone wolf on occasion. The pervasive communism of army life always rendered some degree of 'aloneness' essential to my peace of mind, so that I did not find the present situation irksome. In any case there had been heavy casualties to our platoon since I had joined the 11th Battalion the preceding

May, and I had already become an older member, who was *persona grata* with my companions, many of whom were later additions to our company.

Rampton, with whom I made the bread-scrounging expedition, was one of those whom I had known distantly for some time. He was, if I recollect aright, a chemist's assistant in civil life and educationally rather above our average. I found him a quiet, companionable type, but he came and went mysteriously and was very much a bird of passage. I never remember his going into the trenches. He had rejoined us out of the blue just before our departure from France; he was to disappear again in the near future, though I do not recollect his going. He often reported sick, and I suspect that he had sufficient knowledge and possibly some fortunate misfortune which always enabled him to get away from us in good time.

During the next few days, which were spent on the normal parades and marches into the country, we gradually became used to our new surroundings. The flat surrounding district would have been monotonous had it not been for the sun, the strangeness of the architecture and the beauty of the vineyards, still so green in the late autumn. There were, too, stimulating touches of local colour, exemplified by the massive oxen, hitched to a laden fodder-cart or drawing across tree-bordered fields some primitive farm machine. Sometimes in our military peregrinations we passed an Italian military guard and were shocked at its slackness, the sentries often using their rifles as supports and only awakening to interest at our sudden appearance. Always, from the large houses that studded the countryside, we were welcomed by waving hands. On more than one occasion a lone, dark-shawled, female figure, standing at one of the windows, sometimes young, often older, wiped away tears she was unable to suppress, poignantly reminding us of the tragedy that this fair land had been enduring. From the beginning of their war in 1915, the Italian casualties had been unusually heavy.

It was very cold at night and we were glad, after a day or two, to receive a second blanket for our beds upon the floor. At 6.30 am we had to be ready for physical jerks on the lawn to tune us up for the day. It was very cold until the sun came up, dispersing the early frost that rose in a curtain-like haze from the ground. Each time that miraculous transformation scene dazzled me with wonder.

At first the meagre military ration of bully beef and hard biscuits left us hungry, a hunger we were unable to assuage by purchases as in France; but shortly this British food was supplemented by Italian rations. Not that we were as grateful as we should have been. The butter and bacon were putrid; the meat, we declared, must have been old bullock killed by overwork. Only the closely-woven and somewhat dry Italian army bread was both plentiful and edible. What would we not have given for a real steak and mashed potatoes!

At a pay parade, in usual style from a table placed in front of the house, in the presence of Captain Stirling, whom we saluted before and after in regulation manner, I received twenty lire (equivalent to ten shillings and a useful sum in those days). We were officially warned that Italian *vino rosso* was much more potent than French *vin rouge*, a warning that was both ignored and amply justified that evening when a number of the company, normally inured to strong liquor, came back not drunk but very sick and ill.

There was great excitement on the night of 17 November when the first post from Blighty caught up with us, and those of us who received mail, somewhat delayed though it was, were accounted fortunate. We had been advised that our correspondence should be addressed to the Italian Expeditionary Force and had derived a good deal of satisfaction from this evidence of our special assignment, which was not among those details to be kept from our folks at home.

The following day, being Sunday, commenced with church parade and also brought the news that we were to move off the next day. Already boxes of Mills bombs and Very lights, the usual harbingers of action, had arrived in quantity at company stores and we knew that our brief spell of leisure was ending. The division was under orders to enter the battle zone.

A steam-tram connected the village with Mantua. Like a miniature train, it puffed incongruously along the high road and suddenly decided to take a short-cut across the fields. The city was out of bounds. We could not therefore board the tram. It seemed, however, a pity not to gain a second glimpse of this interesting place, and as it had become generally known that the pickets could easily be evaded I decided to join Rampton and another man in an evening trip to the city. As the latter was one of our corporals, I felt that I should at least be erring in good company. After tea we three set off with some trepidation. Our plan was to reach the main railway line at a road crossing and to proceed on foot along the permanent way. This, we understood, would enable us to evade the military police patrols, which kept to the main road.

That Sunday evening Mantua was a sight to see. The main streets were thronged with men in British uniforms, mostly officers or men of the supply and headquarter services. Our chief danger was that we might bump into one of our own officers, and we kept a wary look out as we joined the motley throng of Italians and Britons. Already our service corps had settled in and made themselves at home. British traffic police had taken over from the Italian civilian authorities. They were wearing a type of slouch hat similar to that worn by the Australians, and we were pleased to hear that it was intended to substitute this for our ordinary service cap while we were in Italy. Whatever truth there may have been in this report, it was not to materialise. In the army normal custom was not easily altered.

The crowds on the sidewalks included a fair sprinkling of Italian soldiers, the rankers dressed in ill-fitting uniforms of a drab greenish grey cloth, in great contrast to the officers, whose smart well-cut blue uniforms with white facings appeared almost feminine to us. Among the civilians, particularly the women, the predominating garb was black. This fashion had the effect of enhancing, in vivid contrast, the picturesque beauty of the city's medieval architecture in the setting sun.

We had no particular objective. The real success of the evening would depend upon our reaching and leaving the forbidden territory without discovery, and I saw no reason to quarrel with my companions' unoriginal suggestion that we should have a drink. We entered a wine shop, of which there were many, all doing a roaring trade, and found it a very different sort of establishment from our pub at home. There was an ordinary shop-counter in front of a tier of shelves crammed with an incredible array of bottles, many of which had already been opened. My companions were as ignorant as I was of the specific delights that the labels of those bottles indicated, and we selected one marked *cognac*, which seemed to have a certain familiarity. We ordered three by the simple expedient of showing three fingers. We could certainly have done much better than choose brandy, which fortunately was not of a very strong variety, for we drank it neat. Neither of my companions was out for a booze and, honour being satisfied, we returned to our billet without incident, well pleased with our farewell trip to the historic city.

2: ACROSS THE PLAINS OF LOMBARDY

On Monday 19 November 1917, following reveille at 3.30am, we made our final arrangements for the great march. First the billets had to be cleaned up and left in good order. This had always been the army's policy, but on this occasion even more attention was being given to it. The evidence of an Italian officer, which was transmitted at the time by the British Ambassador in Rome to the Foreign Secretary, is worth quoting. Referring to the British troops, he wrote:

> They are marvellous. I am not speaking of their discipline, which is perfect, but of the singular delicacy of feeling which distinguishes officers and soldiers. When they leave a billet which they have occupied not a chair is out of its proper place. Their cleanliness is so great that you would not find a straw on the ground. So with their camps, where hundreds of wagons and quadrupeds have stopped; they do not leave any trace of their passage. No one even takes a glass of water without leave.

A little flowery perhaps, but this was certainly the impression we tried to leave.

On our arrival in Italy we had been admonished to keep smart and emulate the Guards. During the preceding days much spit and polish had been expended. We were now expected to create an impression, to inspire confidence in the people, who were to see and hear about the Allied contingents marching with drums beating and fifes playing in smartly-uniformed and well-aligned columns of four, towards the field of battle. Never before had our soldierly mission figured so prominently in our minds, and we were indeed proud to be the chosen representatives of Britain in this land, so different from anything we had previously seen. It is certainly a pity that we did not know it at the time — for such knowledge would have helped us to bear with rather better grace some of the irksome details of our experience — that the operation had been so organised that our line of march was one of a series of parallel routes towards the Piave line. In conjunction with our other brigades and with the French troops, we could, in case of emergency, be rapidly deployed to meet a further enemy penetration.

The operation began at 7 am through Mantua, where we marched past a group of important-looking brass hats, and out on to the Padua road. This was one of those straight probing causeways raised slightly above the level of the countryside, which spreads out on either side like a ground-plan, everchanging in detail but of a monotonous flatness that quickly becomes uninteresting. The road itself was surfaced with a fine white dust that soon covered our boots and equipment, spoiling all our earlier efforts to make them sparkle. Occasionally we passed through a village, though as often as not we left it away to the right or the left, where it stood aloof from the route, which had been designed with Roman precision to join the more important places, but which took little heed of the lesser communities that did not lie in the exact line. These communities join up to the highway by narrow side-turnings and the effect is interesting. Each place has its own campanile — a square detached tower standing near the church and marking the presence of habitations well ahead of the route. These independently-standing bell-towers contrasted strangely with our spires and steeples at home, a survival from the ages when the bell not only called the faithful to prayer but also sounded the tocsin in times of trouble, which were rarely absent in the chequered history of Lombardy and Venetia.

The sun shone all the way, and in the far distance we could discern the fringe of mountains, which seemed to recede as we stepped towards them. Distances were hard to judge in the clear atmosphere. After marching twenty kilometres, a fatiguing experience with our heavy packs and their recent additions, we were glad to fling our burdens aside, but we were disappointed to discover that the only available sleeping place was the open field alongside the road. This was somewhere in the neighbourhood of the village of Castel d'Arno.

Some attempt was made to provide us with shelter, for it was here that we made our first acquaintance with the Italian army bivouac, which their troops carried in sections. Each bivouac, shared among four men, consisted of four pieces of blue waterproof canvas, which could be buttoned together, and a similar number of wooden sections so shaped as to form into a central tee-piece. To us the contraption was a jigsaw puzzle, the selection and buttoning of which was most confusing. Even when we managed to produce a complete four-sided shelter, the tee-pieces usually proved insufficient to raise it on high. Only a few tents were destined to be raised in that field, most of us deciding to cut our losses and use the canvas sections as bed coverings. But it proved a bitterly cold night and I spent most of the time on my feet or sharing a fire lit by an enterprising member of the company.

It was hardly surprising therefore that we were not very sprightly when we marched off again at 7.15 on the following morning, and the somewhat shorter march of some sixteen kilometres was to prove no less tiring than that of the day before. At the outset we resorted to song, always a good way of heartening a weary column, and for the first time the wide-eyed but appreciative peasants in the fields stopped working to hear the strains of *Keep the Home Fires Burning* and *Take me back to Dear Old Blighty*, sung with gusto if not always in strict tune. I do not mention *Tipperary*, since there was at this stage of the war a certain diffidence in singing this refrain, owing probably to the sentimentality caused by journalists' reports of its adoption as a sort of anthem by the Old Contemptibles in 1914. But on this day our spirits soon began to flag and the music died away. Our packs were weighing heavily and we had casualties, who were picked up by the Red Cross cart trailing along in the rear. The officers did all they could to prevent this, threatening malingerers with dire penalties, but it is not possible to stop a man from falling by the wayside if he is dead beat. Hitherto falling out on marches had never become a habit, though many of our new members from the service corps had had little marching experience. The absence of any real malingering was more or less endorsed by the fact that no penalties were subsequently imposed. The battalion's band certainly helped a lot to keep up our flagging spirits but unfortunately, at the tail of the column, which was 'B' Company's position that day, the drum beat arrived late and contributed something to the confusion.

The countryside continued very much as before. Everywhere the irrigation ditches ran with the clearest water. Here and there we saw women industriously washing garments in the streams. Without soap they banged the saturated clothes against the wooden boards on which they usually knelt, or even against bare stones, and their vigorous efforts achieved a vivid whiteness as the garments dried in the sun. Again there was little to break the monotony, and the diminutive 'milestones' gained an importance out of all proportion to their size. Each silent sentinel seemed to be further away from its predecessor as the day wore on. We were glad to reach our destination, a small hamlet, where we were billeted in a medium-sized house, in which we were crammed with barely sufficient space to lay out our blankets. But, after all, this was a great improvement on the day before. It was my bad luck to be allocated mess-orderly duties and I found little opportunity to rest my weary limbs before bedtime. During the evening there was one brave sight to hearten any expatriate warrior. In the small courtyard before the house sacks and sacks of mail had been deposited, the post of many days having caught up with us. At least a dozen letters and packages were to fall to my lot, an addition to the next day's pack to which I certainly had no objection. By 8 pm we were getting between our blankets, for orders had been issued for reveille at 2.30 am.

We slept heavily on that all-too-brief night and by 4 am on 21 November our blankets had been rolled in tens for transport, breakfast served and the billets cleaned up. The day was beginning to break as we marched through the large village of Cerea. We were ordered to keep quiet, and nothing could be heard but the regular tramp of marching feet. I flashed my pocket lamp on the shuttered windows as we passed. Suddenly an upper shutter flew back and the white-shrouded form of an old lady, holding a candle aloft, stood out in the beam of light. A roar of laughter ran down the column as the flustered figure hastily withdrew. How strange must that experience have seemed to her and probably to other inhabitants of that obscure Italian village, to awaken to the passing of an alien column with its unbroken tramping re-echoing through the deserted street as it marched away towards the rising sun.

The roads were coated with a thin layer of ice, on which our heavy boots slid hither and thither, making it difficult to avoid falling. The air was chill at that early hour but refreshing, and we made good progress in the early stages. The sun came up gradually from behind the mists which hung about the fields at daybreak, dissolving the haze as its warming rays shone down upon the white surface of the road. It was all so new to us, and in November too!

Our new platoon commander, marching at the head of his men, used the opportunity to make himself agreeable with those about him. Not that he had any difficulty in this, for he was a slightly built, nervous type, certainly not cut out for a soldier, who would have found it extremely difficult to domineer in any circumstance. He seemed to be overawed by his responsibility, as well he might be (though so few in his position were) and his piping voice, which in command seemed to be rising to a rush of tears, made him the butt of much kind-hearted humour. He was so clearly a fish out of water and also an intelligent man that I wondered why he had taken on the responsibilities of leadership in the infantry. I felt really sorry for him and could never find it in my heart to laugh at his pathetic attempts to wear the mantle of authority, which the King's Regulations so firmly fixed upon his narrow shoulders.

The halt for dinner, alongside the straight stretch of *pavé*, was very welcome. Then we could resort to our water bottles, a solace not permitted during the short regulation halts, although many subterfuges were adopted to evade the restriction. There was little cover in the neighbouring field, lying as flat as a billiard table below the level of the road, but during that halt the value, if not the beauty, of its soil was increased by the calls of nature, which a proportion of the company found imperative at that leisure moment. Modesty receives short shrift on such occasions, which characterise the inconveniences of army life not usually mentioned in the history books, though none the less real for all that.

When we took the road again the sun had become oppressive. Halt followed halt, and tiredness gained an increasing grip upon the moving column. The afternoon was well advanced but still our destination, wherever it might be, did not materialise. We marched through Bevilacqua, another place with a castle. There had been more casualties. Many were lagging, silently struggling over difficult steps. We tried a song, but the front ranks finished it alone. The sun and the weight were relentlessly getting us down. Then we came to a bend in the road and unexpectedly the band in front struck up. A few hundred yards ahead a town came suddenly into view, but no ordinary town. There before us lay a medieval fortress with crenelated battlements, watch towers and drawbridge, like an engraving from a Scott novel. It was a miraculous sight and had a miraculous effect. The ranks closed as if by magic. No longer was it necessary for the NCOs to bawl themselves hoarse to keep stragglers from the wrong side of the road. Men whose backs had been gradually bending under the strain became erect. I experienced an unaccountable increase in strength: the whole company seemed rejuvenated.

We were brought to attention. And so, in perfect order, we marched towards this vision of the past — the city of Montagnana. Never shall I forget my first glimpse of those wonderful walls, bathed in the reddening glow of the afternoon sun. It was as though we had been suddenly transported back into history, and I was thrilled by the sense of romance that had for ever departed from the trappings of war. I saw the mail-clad warriors of other ages assembled before a town of dreams, and wondered, as we approached the picturesque gateway, how such a sight could possibly survive into our mundane age. Here was a picture for an artist, or even for a photographer — though I fear neither was present — a modern detachment of one of Britain's greatest regiments, marching into an Italian town, whose very stones exuded the story of the centuries. I felt humble, and any inclination to rebel was stilled within me.

The head of the battalion approached the lowered drawbridge, now thronged with townsfolk eager to welcome us, and with band playing we marched past a detachment of the Italian garrison, drawn up at the salute, through the battlements into the town. It was like entering another world. Montagnana, though in the twentieth century an inconspicuous place, could boast one of the finest medieval walls in Europe. As I was subsequently to learn, outside the famed tourist centres of whose abundance Italy can justly be proud, there are a multitude of such lovely retiring places to delight the less orthodox traveller.

That day we had covered some 28 kilometres, a good march in the circumstances. 'B' Company's billet was in a sort of store-room on the first floor of a building in one of the main streets. It was a loft constructed of red terracotta bricks, which left a pinkish dust on everything that came into contact with them. With a series of large brick pillars supporting its low ceiling, it was spacious enough to house the whole company. No sooner had we cast aside with heartfelt relief our burdensome equipment than the order was given to remove our puttees, boots and socks for foot inspection by the officer, who detailed some to attend the Medical Officer for treatment. My feet were blistered, but not badly enough to call for special attention.

After tea we went out to have a look round. The old city lived up to our first impressions. We gazed with wonder upon its impressive walls and the old surrounding moat, now dry. We explored the dark connecting passages which threaded the older parts and we had no difficulty in imagining the dark cloaked figures of conspirators and footpads, who had surely lurked in these shadows in times gone by. On our way back we were drawn by a rich red glow reflecting intermittently upon the ramparts, accompanied by the crackle of musketry. Imagining all kinds of impossible things, we hastened with many others to the spot, only to come upon a utilitarian incinerator in full blast, into which the Italians had foolishly deposited quantities of small-arms ammunition, which fortunately were exploding piecemeal.

I was impressed above all else by the wonderful supplies of fruit displayed on stalls and in the shops, especially the large bunches of luscious grapes, so cheap that they could hardly be resisted. The shopkeepers were doing a roaring trade with their khaki-clad visitors. We came upon the fine cathedral, whose highly embellished interior rather belied the austere exterior. It happened that a funeral service was in progress and the entire church was ablaze with lighted candles, which, with the chanting of choir and the smell of incense, contributed to an impressive scene. What a contrast to the obsequies of the battlefield!

Hereabouts we ran into Rampton, bursting to tell someone about his recent adventure. He had entered a shop to make a purchase, and the shopkeepers — a man and a woman — had invited him into a room at the rear to take coffee. They were pleasantly interested in his uniform and he was impressed by their kindness. All this communicating had gone on despite a mutual lack of common words. Then the woman had invited him to follow her upstairs. She was of uncertain age, but that is hardly significant in the hard-working south, and there was little doubt as to her intention. Surprised and not a little frightened, Rampton had wished his sudden friends a hasty goodbye, and had almost straightaway blundered into us. Laughingly telling him that some people got all the luck, we returned to billet to turn over in our minds the effect that uniforms have upon the morals of people. Secretly I envied Rampton his slight adventure, knowing full well that I should have reacted just as he had, and have been rather shamefaced about it. We had not been brought up to figure out logically the actual basis and intentions of our sexual impulses, which of course were further deflected and suppressed by the exigencies of army life.

By 8 am on the following morning we were on the road again. Shortly we began to enter rougher country. Low hills bordered the route, which kept strictly to the valley. During the morning we passed detachments of Italian troops, obviously belonging to the divisions involved in the retreat from Caporetto, who were no doubt being withdrawn to the back areas for reorganisation and re-equipment. Indeed they needed it. Scantily garbed, many only half-clothed, with dirty and torn uniforms, unshaven and blear-eyed, these exhausted soldiers, whose appearance contrasted so with our sedulously-encouraged smartness, were to be pitied. Their transport was perhaps the most revealing feature: a miscellaneous collection of nonmilitary carts and waggons of all shapes and sizes, crammed with objects of a domestic character, here an iron bedstead with a bundle of bedding, there a tin bath, a few chairs, with domestic animals intermixed. Soldiers walked in front leading half-starved horses, a calf, some sheep. Other soldiers, less energetic even, slouched along behind, toes showing through their broken boots. It was a sight for tears. On the appearance of the first shabby detachment a cruel derisive voice shouted, 'Here comes Sanger's Circus', and with a roar of thoughtless laughter 'Sanger's Circus' it was henceforth to be. We were sorry, but we laughed.

After a good midday rest we marched through picturesque little Barbarano, with its inevitable castle, set amidst the hills, and reached our new billet, whose name I did not note, at 4 pm. Our unpretentious little building had an unusual amenity in a small spring by the roadside, which gave forth a constant stream of hot water, a boon for which we were extremely grateful. It led to a good deal of discussion during the evening. It seems that this geyser-like phenomenon was of volcanic origin, and certainly the surrounding hills had a wild chaotic look which suggested some sort of gigantic upheaval many ages ago. Though we did not know it at the time, we were in the Berici Mountains, a sort of detached island of extinct volcanoes of modest height springing from the plains due south of the artistic city of Vicenza.

Those billets had recently been used by Italian troops. Across the road under the shadow of the hill there was a sight that contrasted pointedly with our own British methods of achieving good sanitary standards. There, clear for all the world to see, were their abandoned latrines: no order, no privacy, literally a field of filth. I had never seen such a disgusting sight and wondered what kind of epidemic was being bred amidst the excreta and soiled paper.

During the next few days our march seemed to lose its original precision. At least, after spending a night at a place called Montegaldella, I lost trace of our wanderings. The embargo on the purchase of bread was reinforced with due warnings, and our rations, owing no doubt to our mobility, had become too scanty to sustain the energies needed for marching. Dried figs from a sort of grocer's shop was the only treasure-trove to reward our scourings in Montegaldella. A day or two later we encountered *polenta* for the first time and helped down a dish of this cold batter-like substance with a cup of red wine. We were to discover better ways of enjoying it. For a couple of days fog came down on the plain and we felt the cold. On the evening of 24 November we heard for the first time the distant rumble of artillery, and knew that we were nearing the line.

Then the sun came out again, disclosing in all their glory the snow-clad mountains beyond the edge of the plains, now much nearer than before. The day's marches had been shortened so that we could carry a blanket rolled upon our packs, and we arrived much more exhausted. We stopped at one uninteresting billet for a couple of nights, while rumour about our future movements beat upon us with the arrival of every stranger from outside the company. The roads were becoming congested with cross-traffic, and our halts — to allow convoys to cross the route — became more and more frequent. One night we stopped at a nameless village whose signposts pointed mountainwards to Bassano. Our billet was a spacious loft, which had but one small window and was reached through a small door about a dozen feet from the ground by means of an iron ladder. On first seeing this shelter some of the company demurred at entering, preferring to put down their kits in the draughty courtyard. This was vetoed, and incipient revolt petered out. As was customary we lit our way to slumber by means of candles, in this case stuck precariously on the crossbeams above the hay which covered the floor. If one had fallen we would not have had a dog's chance of survival. But the resilience of youth prevented such fears from spoiling a good night's sleep, and I awakened whole and refreshed. Yet in retrospect I am amazed at the inconsequence of the authorities who permitted such risks to be taken.

On 29 November we reached the weightily battlemented town of Castelfranco Veneto, where we were assigned as billet a large shed on the town's outskirts. I was immensely impressed by the massive castle that dominated the centre of the town, with a fine clock tower on which was sculptured a large representation of the Lion of St Mark. This Venetian sign looking down upon the half-deserted place added a truly fantastic touch to the scene. Many of the townsfolk had fled. Those who remained seemed to spend much of their time queuing outside the *panificio* for bread. After dark all lights were turned low for fear of air raids. We were definitely in the war zone.

Our sick parades were increasing, probably on account of the poor rationing. I felt unwell but not sufficiently so to report sick. Some relief came on 1 December, when we were cheered by the issue of a small ration of white bread from the army bakehouse, our first since leaving France. At Castelfranco we came into contact with Italian troops billeted in the neighbourhood. As usual they evinced great interest in the technicalities of our equipment, which they clearly regarded as superior to their own, though I doubt now whether it was always as suitable as theirs for the sort of fighting in which they had been involved. Many of them spoke English well but with an American accent, for numbers had returned from the United States to fight for their fatherland. No one could accuse the Italians of a lack of patriotism. With this satisfactory characteristic I was inclined to contrast, and not to our advantage, our own constant grousings, which would certainly have amazed and possibly have misled them. There may have been doubts about our ally's staying power, particularly at that juncture, but I had nothing but admiration for their obvious enthusiasm.

3: THE MONTELLO FRONT

The division now went into the line. On 2 December we marched through Montebelluna to the village of Biadene, a couple of miles beyond, where we took over the reserve positions. Montebelluna, which we were to get to know quite well, was an open township of modern construction nestling amidst the foothills, and had until quite recently been a thriving community on the main route into the mountains. Many of its inhabitants had fled before the unexpected tide of war, but some civilians were hanging on hopefully to look after their possessions or to keep open the few shops; though there was little to be bought, certainly not bread, which was our greatest need. The place had an abandoned air, which, to some extent, was being accentuated by the superimposition of alien military establishments. These occupied the municipal buildings, including the now forlorn little theatre, so typical of Italian provincial culture. There was a half-built modern church, on which work had presumably been suspended at the outbreak of war, and the electric trams no longer rattled over the *pavé* streets. Yet there was still an air of acute respectability about the place.

The great retreat had ended along the Piave river, whose right bank had been held by the Italians from the mountains across the Lombardian plain down to the Adriatic Sea near Venice. Our main defensive position was the long mole-shaped Montello hill, with the river beyond its further slopes standing between us and the Austrians. Westwards to our left, where the Piave issued from the mountains, the line swung by the strong positions of Monte Tomba and Monte Grappa, and thence all the way through the Alps to the tip of Lake Garda, on which the whole Austro-Italian line had for long rested. The Montello was therefore an eminently defensible key-position more or less in the centre of the line where mountain and plain met. The hill itself is some seven miles long, broadening to four miles at its widest and rising to about 800 feet, a pleasant hill, covered with vineyards and cultivated fields, interspersed with small woods, and containing depressions and narrow clefts at the top, which at the time provided good artillery positions. The northern slopes fell steeply to the riverbank, above which in places they towered like cliffs. The Montello also offered a series of effective observation posts over the enemy positions beyond the river, at least 800 yards away, and right up to the foothills of the Alps. But beyond those hills, where the pine-clad mountains towered into the sky, the observational advantages were all with the enemy. At the outset there was little to cause our observers sleepless nights, for, as it was reported in the *Official History*[1], 'In early December, no appearance of fife could be observed there, rarely was a gun heard, and not a shell hole was to be seen'. Our new enemies had much to learn — and so, indeed, had we.

The position now being taken over by the two British divisions stretched from Pederobba, well to the left of the Montello, to just beyond Nervesa at the right end of the hill, the 41st Division being on the right and ourselves on the left. The enemy positions hereabouts were held by the Austrian 13th Division and the German 12th Division, but within a few days the latter was replaced by the German 11th Division. On our side the 41st had begun to relieve the Italian 1st Division

---

[1] *Military Operations, Italy 1915-1919*, compiled by Brigadier-General Sir James E. B. Edmonds and Major-General H. R. Davies, (HMSO, 1949).

on 30 November and we were now following suit with the Italian 30th Division. Each of our divisions put two brigades in the line, which in each case was held by two battalions in front, one in support and one in reserve. Our battalion was occupying the reserve position of the left-hand brigade of the left division. Two days after our arrival Lord Cavan formally took charge of the British sectors with his headquarters at Fanzolo, four miles north-east of Castelfranco. On 3 December the French had begun taking over Italian positions away in the mountains to our left, an Italian brigade under their control being placed in the line as the connecting link between the two armies.

By all accounts the change-over was a much more pleasant experience than similar occasions in Flanders had been. There were no shells, and the headquarter billets were usually unshattered houses, often standing nakedly above the trenches. In some cases, it is said, barrels of wine were handed over as trench stores! The *Official History* throws an interesting sidelight on a somewhat slap-happy way of conducting war, even after a Caporetto: 'Another difficulty experienced in cooperating with the Italians was their habit of closing down from 12 to 3 pm every afternoon for the midday meal and rest, a habit continued even when the war was not going too well for them; as the Austrians knocked off at 11.30 am for a couple of hours the cause did not suffer. As noon approached Italian officers very obviously became uneasy and wanted to stop any work in hand.' All this would soon be changed.

There was certainly nothing in the atmosphere of the Montello hinterlands early in December to suggest that our position had any element of instability in it. In Biadene, then a collection of whitewashed farms and deserted dwelling houses straggling along the road, Number 6 Platoon occupied the

47

second floor of one of the houses, each section having a small room to itself. In front rose the slopes of the Montello, covered on this side with prosperous-looking farms, while at our back, from the far side of the field behind the house, a low ridge rose clifflike to a height of a couple of hundred feet, the intervening space being covered with crops of uncut maize, now looking somewhat bedraggled. The road from Montebelluna led past the house up the valley, where it opened out funnel-wise towards the river, beyond which the mountains towered up, their pine-clad slopes rising majestically in the clear atmosphere. It was not easy to imagine these heights being in the hands of the enemy, who was in a position to observe almost everything that happened in the village. Compared with the awful forward areas in France, this was a situation of sylvan peacefulness, and, if our above-ground exposure at first seemed positively indecent, we soon got used to it. The main activity on the enemy side seemed to be the creation of fires in the woods. Smoke and flame were continually issuing from some spot or other on the mountainside. After dark the Austrians embellished the scene by switching on searchlights to observe the riverbed. These swept the sky and shingle methodically throughout the night.

We were soon back at our old drill routines and inspections, even skirmishing across the fields towards the line openly. This was, no doubt, not without interest to the Austrian observers who, had they wished, could have brought a sense of reality to our manoeuvres at any time. The Lewis gun teams began to mount anti-aircraft guards, a necessary but free-and-easy duty without the irksomeness of the ceremonial guard. For rifle practice we used the small range of the civilian rifle club, under the sign *Tiro a Segno* situated down the road, and it was while acting as marker at the butts there that I had my first glimpse of a vicious-looking scorpion, scrabbling in the dust.

In order to give our mobile field kitchen a rest, a team of bricklaying experts, assembled for the purpose, built brick ovens in the courtyard of the house. Not that there was at the time much to employ the oven upon. Our rations were still meagre enough, and we were long past being even tired of the eternal bully beef stew. Adding to our diet was a continuing spare-time occupation, but there was little enough to be had. I did manage to buy some Italian chocolate in Montebelluna, at 4 lire (2s) for a small packet, but even at that exorbitant price supplies soon gave out. One such expedition, which proved fruitless as far as food was concerned, found us, by means of a zigzagging path amidst dense shrubs, in a half-inhabited place right on top of the hill behind the billet. Nor was the effort completely without reward, for from the cliff edge we were able to enjoy a magnificent panorama over the Piave river spreading out in numerous streams, its rushing waters like green ribbons flowing over a wide belt of barren stony land. On the far side, where the forested mountain slopes dipped almost to the river-bank, were clusters of white buildings and townlets, all of which were in enemy hands. Gazing upon that lovely scene, peacefully resting in the afternoon sun, it was difficult to believe that down there below us two powerful armies stood face to face, wondering about the morrow.

One of the fruits of these foraging expeditions was the stimulation of interest in the Italian language, and in this I was brought nearer to Isaac Doniger, with whom I was destined to strike up a life-long friendship, which would surmount the geographical separation of his emigration to America after the war. We both resolved to take our studies seriously and had already written home for the dispatch of a set of Hugo's text books in the language, a paperback series very popular at that time.

An important discovery at this juncture enabled some of us to ameliorate the food shortage. In a large house along the road in the direction of the river we discovered a peasant woman, apparently living on her own, an independent soul who had insisted upon staying behind. She made *polenta*, a staple article of food which I have already mentioned, and was prepared to sell it. Her large kitchen, with its open fireplace standing upon a raised base, its wooden-beamed ceiling and floor of rough tiles, one could have imagined as having been transported from Elizabethan England, poor certainly, but kept spotlessly clean. The scanty furnishings consisted of a heavy table, two rickety straight-backed chairs and a plain chest of antique appearance.

With curiosity I watched the housewife at her cooking. A quantity of *farina*, maize flour, from the chest was mixed with water in the pot and stirred slowly over the fire. And that was about all there was to it. At a certain stage she threw in a handful of powder taken from a bin, otherwise the *polenta* literally made itself. When ready it was turned out on a board, a steaming yellow mass looking like boiled batter pudding, and after cooling sufficiently it was cut with a piece of string, just as the grocer used to cut cheese with wire. This *polenta* was somewhat doughy and alone it was poor stuff, but helped out with jam, of which we were rarely short, or added in lumps to thicken the eternal bully beef stew, it made a fair substitute for bread. Many of us found this a handy standby, but there were others in the ranks who would not have it at any price, a reaction that always surprised me considering the poor stuff many of them must have had to put up with at home.

There was one shortage of the moment that put the majority of my companions into agonies of torment — the lack of cigarettes. The Italian brands, they said, were indifferent enough when they were to be had, but soon the company was reduced to smoking dried tea leaves. Fortunately a first army issue was made on 10 December, bringing excitement and relief that magically removed the gloom which had settled upon almost everyone.

On the same day the war on our front opened with the whistling over of two enemy shells into Montebelluna. During succeeding days shells occasionally dropped in our vicinity, but they were absurdly light in calibre. We had no cause to complain, for our own batteries were already beginning to liven things up on Western Front lines. As a consequence we were set to dig slip trenches behind the billet for use in case of serious counter-bombardment. The only casualty in the area that we heard about during those early days was a half-witted youth we had seen about the village. He received a slight shell splinter in the hand and went around looking very proud of himself.

The Dumps, our divisional concert party, established themselves in the town, a cinema was opened, and even a canteen installed, although this had sold out by the time I could get there — and we were only just in the middle of December. The organisers of this praiseworthy effort to keep up morale certainly deserved credit, though I do not recollect that at the time we were very grateful. Even the rations were beginning to improve. But, with the wearing off of our initial excitement at coming to Italy and the recent cessation of purposeful activity, it must be admitted that some boosting of morale was needed. It may be that it was the breaking of the weather and the covering of the countryside with a glistening blanket of snow, giving our surroundings a traditional English Christmas-card look, that put the finishing touch to our depression. The future, despite our modest comfort, began to look hopeless again, the war to assume its normal guise of an endless stream of boredom and slaughter. I know that we had great compensations in our new situation and that we were ungrateful to forget so soon the incredible horror we had left behind in France. In me this feeling had been accentuated by the scene of absolute loveliness which had followed the break from the dry weather. In the morning after the first rain the sun came up clearly, causing the mountains to stand out in chiselled glory against a deep blue sky, and all the slopes were clothed with a virgin whiteness that took my breath away, so grand was the sight. At about this time in the middle of the month our front-line troops had begun to probe into the enemy positions beyond the river, even bringing back a prisoner.

On 19 December orders came for us to take over in the line, and that same afternoon we had a visit from HRH the Prince of Wales. It was well known that the Prince was ever eager to get into the firing line and very understandable that the staff were equally concerned to keep him out of harm's way. We had heard that he had already been in our vicinity during the march from Mantua, but it was not easy to identify personalities among the brass hats who had appeared from time to time as we moved across the country — not that the Prince was difficult to distinguish. Now he certainly did arrive outside the billet, showing a particular interest in our new brick-built cookhouse and other changes wrought during our short stay. Possibly this had been one of the main intentions. From afar he appeared to be keenly interested, but almost overwhelmed by the crowd of bigwigs who hovered about his slight form, seeming from a distance to be steered by the sheer weight of their presence. He certainly had my sympathy, and my feeling was that had I been in his place, which heaven forbid, I would have sent them all packing.

We left billets at 5.30 pm with full pack and rolled blanket for the front-line positions. The journey was uneventful and quite unlike anything we had previously experienced. Number 6 Platoon took over the front trench, with the rest of the company in close support. Carved into the riverbank, the trench was deep and well constructed with orthodox fire-step, bays and dugouts. The support positions were in houses standing sheer on the bank a hundred yards or so behind us, with the windows facing the enemy boarded over to mask the fight at night, and no other precaution. The position seemed too ridiculous, as the enemy, though far away with the river in between, had perfect observation. As if to emphasise the possibilities, one of the houses had a large round hole drilled right through by the passage of a small shell that had not burst upon impact — the only sign of offensive action in the neighbourhood. With our recent experience of the Western Front, which had conditioned us to expect certain military reactions, the atmosphere here seemed unreal and chronically unstable, though it was remarkable how quickly we settled down to the new situation and came to take it for granted.

The view from our trench was magnificent, a panoramic scene of mountain and river filling the entire field of vision. A wide bed of shingle divided us from the enemy, whose trenches on the far bank were at this point three kilometres away. The stony desert was broken occasionally by islands covered with stunted shrubs, among which the Piave flowed in many streams, some mere rivulets, others broad and roaring torrents thrusting through the ribbon-like channels in the shingle. The sound of rushing waters provided a continuous background noise to all our activities. Movements in the Austrian fines were discernible only through field glasses, and only the officers and a few company observers had these. Opposite us the wooded mountain slopes came right down to the river's edge, where a road linked a number of hamlets, which we could clearly see, but to the left the valley narrowed up into the mountains, whose white-capped peaks filled the horizon. In front of this valley, at a place marked 'Vidor' on the map, we could see the shattered arches of a bridge, indicating the main road and rail routes into the Alps, astride of which the two armies now faced each other. Further to the left, where the line bent towards the west, the mountain ridge rose sheer, and at night the lights high up indicated where the Allied positions continued on through the high mountains.

During our first days in the trenches the front remained unnaturally quiet. At night from time to time Austrian searchlights swept the valley and seemed to linger over our positions, but there was little they could have detected there. Behind us the Montello stood out sharply against the clear sky and the world seemed dead. Occasionally a rifle shot rang out from our trenches into the waste, but this practice was soon vetoed as a danger to our own patrols, and shooting from the line was restricted to two practice bursts in daytime from the Lewis guns. The nights were extremely cold, causing us to light up brazier fires inside the dugout, which virtually smoked us out. A light fall of snow found the weak spots in these shelters, which were merely roofed over with light branches, and the dripping conditions inside were extremely uncomfortable until all the snow had cleared from overhead.

Our time was spent in continuing sentry turns; otherwise there would have been little to do but tidy up the trenches and contemplate the scene. One night we scrounged flour from an abandoned house and, aided by the campaigning ingenuity of our Corporal Goffee, who had seen regular service in India, we concocted some quite palatable *polenta* in a mess tin, and were duly proud of our culinary achievement. Not that we were doing too badly for food. The field kitchen, an unusual visitor to the trenches, had been sited just behind one of the houses, whence it served five distinct 'meals' daily. These commenced with gunfire at 3am, breakfast at 7.30am, dinner at 12.30pm, tea at 4 pm and supper at midnight. Two of us went on each occasion to fetch the section's share and, although there was a well-constructed communications trench and we had been warned not to make unnecessary movements in daylight, it was found convenient to carry the containers over the top. We fetched our water from the nearest stream out in front. Rum was issued at 'stand down' in the morning.

As now for the first time in Italy our section constituted an offensive unit the occasion seems opportune to provide details of our up-to-date membership. Corporal Goffee had been our leader since I joined the battalion at Ypres towards the end of the previous May. He was a quietly-spoken, broad-minded, and not too strict leader whose obvious competence and prestige as an old soldier, coupled with a cockney sense of humour, ensured our complete co-operation. In other words ours was an exceptionally happy section. Since my advent we had lost three members in action — two killed and one seriously wounded — a sad but far from disproportionate loss in view of the severity of the battles in the Salient during 1917. There were three others whose service was longer than mine: Westgarth, Wetherall and Hardcastle, close high-spirited companions whose conduct had earned them the label of 'The Three Musketeers'. Westgarth, a Northumbrian miner and champion amateur sprinter, was our Number One on the gun. He was the only private in the platoon who carried a revolver in place of a rifle, his job being to handle the gun in action, under the corporal's orders. Wetherall, a shortish typical Durham miner, was the Number Two, with responsibility for the spare parts; while Hardcastle, tall, gawky and a railwayman in private life, like the rest of us carried the spare magazines with ammunition for the gun. These three were inseparables, invariably arguing and skylarking, often to the corporal's distraction. Gaps had to be filled, and at that time three members from a later draft were attached to the section. Old Tom Ireland, whom I have already mentioned, was the most aged member, who earned his living as a tram driver in Bradford. He had a heart of gold, and was universally liked in the platoon, never presuming that his years entitled him to special privileges. His good temper, fund of experience of life, and common sense made him an ever-welcome companion on sentry turns. During forthcoming Italian nights our tête-à-tête were to found a friendship that was to last right up to the Second World War. There was also a harum-scarum youth named Venus, who had been in the Merchant Navy, and lastly the Polish Jew, already mentioned. The latter was attached to us only temporarily and we were not sorry when authority eventually decided that he had not the makings of a machine-gunner. He was an incredible character. When he received a parcel from home he succeeded in keeping it entirely to himself, without calling forth the slightest protest.

Very soon there were signs that the Allies were taking the offensive. One of our night patrols crossed the river, encountered an enemy detachment and brought back a prisoner. Christmas day came while we were still in the trenches and passed quietly; plum pudding was served. It was so warm in the sun that we could sit round with our shirts off to deal with our vermin. The whole scene — it was not put on record — presented a happy Christmas picture. On Boxing Day the giants stirred. In the quiet sunshine we suddenly became aware of the approach of a large squadron of Gothas, the Germans' latest large bombing planes, accompanied by numerous scouts, sailing towards us from beyond the Piave. That aerial armada looked splendid as it approached with majestic assurance against a background of the brightest blue, and as the smaller machines wheeled the planes shone silver against the sun's rays. It seemed an appropriate occasion for the delivery of our Christmas boxes and we gazed up open-mouthed at the immensity of this unexpected demonstration. But there was a great surprise in store, for us as much as for them. As the enemy planes were nearing the Montello, the front below them suddenly came to life, like an angry giant stirring from a siesta. The British artillery opened up, spattering the sky with shell-bursts, while from the trenches Lewis guns rattled from all directions. The peacefulness had all been a sham: it was as though we had been waiting for just such an opportunity and full advantage was being taken of it. The enemy marauders had indeed lit upon a hornet's nest. They were flying perhaps rather lower than they would normally have done. The armada swung round precipitately and, without delivering their loads, fled back towards the plains over the river. It was soon reported that one had been brought down somewhere in the neighbourhood. Later when we left the trenches we learned that the enemy raid, which had surely been staged as a reprisal for the stepping up of Allied air activity, had been a complete fiasco, a number of aircraft having been lost. From one that had crashed just beyond a hill not far from our billet I was later to retrieve a small piece of aluminium framework as a souvenir.

On the following morning the Austrians made a modest counter-stroke by dropping just one shell alongside a large villa, which was being used as a first-aid post, catching a group of men waiting in apparent security to receive medical attention. Just one shell, and all was quiet again. Another batch of names was added to the list of those who would never return home.

It was at night that the situation in the trenches became tiresome, when the turns of sentry were so cold as to be barely supportable. As in all such static situations, with boredom in control, the smallest incident could provide food for conversation and the flimsiest happening would be dramatised. Thus one of the company's officers, aiming to waken things up a bit, crept up and surprised a sentry post, then played hell at being allowed to draw so close without challenge. This well-justified stratagem was taken very badly by the rank and file, and greatly to everyone's delight the same officer on a subsequent night was frightened out of his skin by a second sentry, who had hidden himself in anticipation at the ruse being repeated, as indeed happened. The retailing of the officer's discomfiture at being suddenly challenged with a bayonet within an inch or so from his middle was sufficiently amusing to keep the company laughing throughout the following day. After this tit-for-tat the situation returned to normal. To such childish depths did boredom often lead us.

On the night of 27 December we went back to reserve billets some way in front of Biadene, at the point where the road bends towards the river. Two platoons shared a cattle shed, the floor of which lay deep in hay, a comfortable and warm if a not too-hygienic bed. The Montello came close to the road thereabouts and a small village a little way in front was occupied by our brigade headquarters. Camouflage strung across the road at intervals went some way towards masking the place from Austrian observation posts in the mountains, which seemed to look straight down on the place. We argued that it could not possibly be so dangerous as it looked, otherwise brigade would not be there! But I think that our comparative safety depended at the time largely upon the very different conception of war still held by the Austrians, who had little of the German ruthlessness.

No sooner had we settled into the new billet than the bulk of the platoon was sent away to join the Staffordshires for a few days on working party. The Lewis gunners were left to mount anti-aircraft guards — an outcome of the revived aerial activity — and we found ourselves with a very pleasant assignment. I was able to bring my mail up-to-date and to make up for the lost sleep of the few days in the line.

At night enemy planes dropped bombs about the countryside, and it began to feel a little like old times on the Western Front. On Sunday afternoon our artillery opened out in fine style, while there was considerable warlike activity up on the ridge away to our left. The enemy brought down one of our observation balloons. We heard later that the French had carried out a successful line-straightening attack, taking 4 field-guns, 60 machine guns and 1,450 prisoners.[2] We spent the last

---

[2] It was not usual for us to receive such detailed information at the time and even less usual, I imagine, for anyone to place it on record. It may therefore be of some interest to note how the *Official History* deals with the incident. It states (p. 117), concerning the successful French attack on Monte Tomba, that they lost 249 killed and wounded and the Austrians over 500 dead and 1,564 prisoners.

day of 1917 in making hurdles, and the rest of the platoon rejoined the company.

'The 41st and 23rd Divisions enjoyed, in comparison with conditions on the Western Front, a fairly quiet time.'[3] This is how the *Official History* succinctly and fairly summarises these closing weeks of an exceptionally long year. The *Official History* also states that the only day during December when shelling rose to the scale of the Western Front was on the 8th of the month. The German 12th Division, before leaving for Germany, had taken the opportunity of firing off all their remaining ammunition. This could not have made much impression on us in the billets in Biadene, where we were at the time, for I made no reference to it in my diary. The *Official History* also refers to bombardment and counter bombardment by our artillery in an endeavour to infuse an offensive spirit into the Italians, but this too must have made little impression on us at the time, with the intensive strafings of the Flanders front still vividly in our minds.

We received during this period the annual number of our divisional magazine *The Dump*, containing topical short humorous stories and articles, rhymes and sketches by Gerald Hudson, Dorothy Heather, Gladys Peto, Byam Shaw and others. This was a professional production which very well interprets the attitudes of the times. As members of the division we were all eager to purchase copies and to send them home as mementoes of our great adventure.

---

[3] *Official History, op. cit.* p. 115.

HISTORICAL NOTE: THE WAR AT THE OUTSET OF 1918

With the Great War now three years and five months old, 1918 opened less hopefully for most of the participants than had any earlier war year. There still seemed to be no end.

1917 had been a year of hammering campaigns and considerable losses. The Germans had failed in their submarine campaign to starve out the British Isles, but had achieved military successes on all the battle fronts where they were involved. The French, after the unsuccessful Battle of Champagne in the spring, had had to cope with near-mutiny in some of their front-line units. The Russians had begun their world-shattering revolution and fighting had stopped on the Eastern Front. The Italians, as we have seen, had escaped disaster by a hair's breadth. The Americans, who had entered the war in the spring, were beginning to build up their new army in France, and their minds at least were not obsessed by visions of previous slaughter. The British had been engaged with varying success on many fronts. After gruelling battles on the Western Front, particularly in the Salient — Messines, Third Ypres and Passchendaele — they had gained a brilliant initial success with a vast tank drive in November at Cambrai, news of which had been welcomed prematurely by the ringing of bells in all the churches of the land, only for this victory to be reversed by the Germans ten days later. The Turks were being hard pressed by the British, whose troops had entered Jerusalem on 11 December.

There were few alive on New Year's Day 1918 who could reasonably foresee the end of the war before 1919. The

Germans, receiving large reinforcements of battle-hardened divisions from the east and under increasing hardship from the British sea-blockade, realised the need to strike with all their might before the arrival of substantial American reinforcements to the Allies. They at least knew that it was victory in 1918 or not at all, and were planning accordingly.

4: MARKING TIME

With the company on holiday, 1918 opened under a sun shining pleasantly down upon a landscape carpeted with sparkling snow, an appropriate setting for a day assigned in belated celebration of Christmas. As if to remind us of the grim reality which we were ever minded to forget, the enemy opened the day by sending over a Gotha loaded with presents that we would hardly have welcomed. But this gesture was frustrated by the responding machine gun fire from the ground and the pursuit of our watchful fighters, who chased the raider back to earth. We were able to laze unmolested in the sunshine and look forward to the meal which both cookhouse and company staff were busily preparing. Needless to say, this was to prove a great success: a meal laid out regally in a large barn, fit for kings. The menu included roast beef and roast pork; potatoes, onions and cabbage; plum puddings (in tins from England), and was completed with rum punch and beer — just an ordinary repast in a mundane world but at the time, and indeed in retrospect, one of the grandest meals I ever enjoyed, a culinary highlight amidst an endless waste of bully beef stew, broken only by the occasional binge on eggs and chips.

On the third day, as our section were preparing for antiaircraft guard, there was a serious accident in the billet; that is if one can use the term 'accident' for what was an act of criminal foolishness on the part of one of our members. There are some who, even with army experience, cannot resist tinkering about with unexploded missiles. This man had found a strange-looking bomb which had been lying about the billet since our arrival. His method of examination was to place the bomb on the ground before him and to hammer it with his entrenching tool. Suddenly there was a loud report and a piercing scream. The fool was fortunate to lose only a hand: had the particular missile been as effective as our Mills bomb or one of those German stick bombs, which we had learned to give a wide berth to, his story would have been very different. A second man was also seriously wounded, while three or four others sitting near were less seriously hurt.

When we mounted guard, which on this occasion was at battalion headquarters and was therefore carried out with due ceremony, we found ourselves in control of the guardroom. Fortunately we were reinforced by members of the military police, for the lock-up was occupied by a particularly difficult customer, whose reputation was known to all of us. He was an Irishman, thickset and certainly no more than five feet tall, a man with no respect for authority, who spent much of his time in 'clink'. Not a very frightening type in ordinary circumstances, he became a fiend whenever he could obtain sufficient strong liquor. It was said that on such occasions the power of half a dozen stalwarts was needed to hold him down. Needless to say he was held in respect by everyone, and nothing was done to add to the punishment which, under army discipline, he had to undergo. He had accumulated so many days detention that his only time of freedom was when he went into the trenches and then, I have no doubt, his offensive spirit could be harnessed to more purposeful ends. My own personal knowledge of the man was limited to this one encounter, which passed off peaceably enough, for our 'mad Irishman' belonged to another company.

From our term of guard we straightway joined our platoon in the trenches. We found them in a new position on the river slightly to the right of the spot we had held previously. On this occasion Number 6 Platoon was in support, occupying houses standing at the side of a road which skirted the ledge above the river. The road itself, which was in full view of the enemy, was camouflaged with strips of loose cloth. Half-concealed stairways led down the face of the ledge into the trenches on the riverbank below. We occupied a large room, which was entered from a courtyard in the rear of the house, the windows of which had been boarded up. Had they wished, the Austrians could have cleared us out in a couple of minutes. At first we felt apprehensive, for the position seemed quite fantastic, but we soon settled down to the new conditions, and in fact found ourselves even more comfortable than we might have been in billets further back. We soon had a brazier roaring away, for which our scrounging parties had no difficulty in finding fuel in the neighbouring houses. Soldiers have little respect for property, particularly when the owners are absent. Abandoned furniture, floorboards and doors, in fact anything combustible that could be removed, was consigned to the flames. Certainly this brazier proved a godsend through the night, when the cold was intense. At stand-to, which lasted for an hour from 6.30 am, we went down to man the trenches and watch the day breaking over the mountains, while the morning air froze the very marrow in our bones. The scene was magnificent; the roar of the torrent drowned all other sounds.

Later the same morning we re-occupied the trenches while our artillery carried out a systematic bombardment of the enemy positions. We watched the shells bursting amidst the small white houses, searching out suspected battery positions, and naturally we expected retaliatory measures from the enemy to deprive us of our own comforts. The Austrians had a reputation for good artillery marksmanship, but that day not a replying shot was fired on our sector. Our afternoon was spent in the warm sunshine at the rear of the billet, letter-writing, dozing, shirt-scouring, and, no doubt, thinking of home, now so far away.

We spent that night from 6 pm in an advanced post on the riverbank, and although we had a dugout of sorts, it was too cold for us to sleep much. Despite the almost continuous daytime sunshine the snow still persisted. On sentry one had to keep moving to maintain one's circulation. This experience was repeated on the following night but one, when the conditions were even worse and the river seemed to be exulting over us in its endless roar.

The snow now turned to rain, spurring the scrounging parties to redouble their efforts. I went out with the wood collectors. We entered the empty riverside houses from the rear. It was already difficult to visualise these derelict habitations as but recently the neat comfortable homes of quiet Italian folk, who had no idea that the tide of war, then so far away and apparently steadily receding with the victories of their men, would suddenly flow back and engulf so much that they held dear. I could visualise them loading up their little carts and hand-barrows with their most cherished belongings and moving reluctantly away upon the arrival of their soldiers. The heavier furniture still remained: a bedstead, a large chest with its contents strewn across the floor, old letters, papers and other odds and ends. We rummaged about in the rubbish, looking at strange stamps, trying to decipher strange writing. A stamp collector myself, I brought away an old letter sheet with a stamp bearing the ancient arms of Austrian Italy. I also extracted from a frame a silk picture on which was printed some sort of encomium. Everywhere there was confusion. Floorboards and skirtings were splintered where they had been hacked by entrenching tools. I imagined with horror the same things happening to my home in Putney. But what was the use of remorse? What we left that day would be garnered on the morrow by someone else, or probably blown to hell by enemy action the day after. That evening the rain turned again to snow.

Good news came from battalion headquarters. Home leave was about to recommence, and we speculated on whose turn would come next. Unfortunately we had all those old soldiers, combed out of the transport and other specialist services, who had joined us before we left France, most of whom had greater seniority than the original infantrymen and would stand ahead of us for leave. In any case, although I had now been abroad for eight months, my turn obviously lay too far ahead for me to derive much anticipatory pleasure. To the ordinary Tommy home leave seemed more than could be deserved, a true gift from the gods. Whenever we heard of someone about to depart to that other mythical world we were filled, not with envy, but with a kind of awe at the very possibility. We were resigned to our fate. The officers went home more frequently but they, we recognised, were of a different clay. The division between the two classes, so effectively perpetuated in the existing King's Regulations, was equally strongly registered in our own consciousness. This is difficult to understand in this later age, but unless it is understood, a true appreciation of what that wartime experience meant to those who participated in it can never be completely achieved. Of course there were the rebels — and some of them have written down their own reactions to the war — but they were few and far between at the time.

On the night of 8 January the company was chosen to send out a patrol to probe the river defences. It was placed under the charge of our platoon commander, and from the team

Westgarth and myself were chosen to handle the Lewis gun. I was not filled with any particular joy at being thus chosen. Divesting ourselves of our uniforms and all possible identification marks, we dressed in white canvas overalls to disguise our forms against the snow. We took neither steel helmet nor box respirator, carrying only our rifles and a single bandolier. Westgarth carried the gun and I spare ammunition. Thus garbed we crossed the trench zone, a party of fifteen in all, white ghosts rather than men, as voices from our advance posts hailed us and without envy wished us the best of luck. It was not a dark night: the bright snow reflected back an unearthly sort of light across the shingle. The cold was intense and we were hardly dressed to cope with it.

Leaving behind our sentries with warnings from them to take care on our return, we waded the first stream, a gliding torrent of icy water not more than a foot deep. Hitherto the scrunchy snow had struck a deep chillness through my boots; now the icy bath penetrated to the skin and took away all feeling from my legs. The previous cold had been warmth compared with this. I walked on, surprised at the noise my absent feet were making as they kicked against the stones. We advanced circumspectly, crossing a number of other small streams, which made their way in separate channels across the riverbed. Here and there patches of stunted bush sprouted up where the ground was higher than the rest, forming more or less permanent islands amidst the shingle. The roar of the torrent now came from all around, for we were literally surrounded by the angry waters. It was a weird and unearthly experience. The cold, biting air reduced feeling almost to naught. We merely knew that we must keep going if we were to save ourselves from merging with the deadness of the surrounding night.

We now reached the most formidable obstacle. A much bigger stream, some thirty yards or so across, now obstructed our progress, and we began with little thought to wade across. It was shallow at first, like the previous streams, but deepened towards the middle. The water was now swirling nearly to our waists. Now surely it would get shallower, but as we approached the opposite bank the waters continued to rise and the current to rush upon us in terrific spate. Taken completely by surprise, I found myself struggling up to my neck. The man just ahead had been swept from his feet and had only just managed to strike the shore where it jutted out into the torrent. I had a similar experience. For a few moments I completely lost my balance and felt myself swirling along helplessly like a cork. It was touch and go, for I was no great swimmer. I saw the bank coming out towards me and then, when right in the grip of the eddy, a hand shot out and I found myself scrambling up the shingle to safety. All this had happened in less time than it takes to describe. It was indeed fortunate for many of us that the current swept us in towards the bank, for a few yards further we should have been shooting out into the main stream. Even as I landed I saw one of our number swimming powerfully. One of the last to cross, he had seen what was happening and had struck out boldly into the waters. His prowess was nearly his undoing, for coming along at a tremendous pace with the current he seemed bound to miss the bank. Fortunately he realised the danger in time and fought strenuously until he reached our landing place. Westgarth had dropped the gun, but it was near the bank and we were able to retrieve it.

We continued forward, more cautiously now, for our misadventure had shaken us quite a little. That swirling stream had to be re-crossed, and if anyone was wounded... Our platoon commander was keeping a good hold on the situation, proving once again that a poor parade-ground soldier, and a diffident soul to boot, could tackle a man's job with credit. The light of the stars, a canopy of brightness such as one rarely sees in our island skies, caused the low bushes to stand out from the snows, and the light, combined with the clatter we were making in the shingle, should have sufficed to disclose our whereabouts to any enemy patrol that might have been nosing around. In truth, though we could not know it at the time, we were quite alone out there.

The noise of the main stream was now becoming audible above all the other sound. The officer, accompanied by an NCO and a runner, went forward to reconnoitre. They were gone but a short while, during which I froze steadily. They had ascertained that the main stream, just a little way ahead, was so swollen by the recent rains and running like a millrace, that it constituted an impassable barrier between us and the enemy. This was why we had not been molested. Glad to be on the move again, we retraced our steps to the previous torrent. After a brief council of war it was decided to form a continuous chain by linking arms and thus to ford the stream. This sensible manoeuvre proved a complete success, at the same time providing valuable experience for the future. Certainly we were swept from our feet as before, but had little difficulty in holding together until we reached the shallows.

How I managed to cover the last part of that journey I do not know. My scanty clothing, soaked with icy water, clung clammily to my numbed body, which no longer had the power to experience anything but an overpowering nothingness. I dimly remember crossing our trenches, hearing detached voices coming out of the unknown, sensing the steps up to the road, and coming into a room where I glimpsed paradise. In that chamber at battalion headquarters a number of receptacles of steaming-hot water gave the interior the appearance of a Turkish bath. Insubstantial khaki figures helped me off with my sodden rags. The hot water immediately began to work. At first it was a kind of pain; then followed a glorious consciousness of returning life. We received clean underclothing, warm blankets and a good tot of rum, and immediately entered into oblivion. With the morning we awoke refreshed and none the worse for our adventure. Nothing had really happened; yet we felt a certain pride at having been chosen for a mission just a little out of the ordinary run of things, a sort of vote of confidence that we were the types that could make it.

During that day, which we spent at headquarters getting our clothing thoroughly dry, the enemy did a little enterprising shooting round the billets, but without causing much damage. They must have been using a type of portable mountain gun, firing what amounted to little more than large explosive bullets.

The same night we joined the company on advance post duties. In the early hours of the morning a fire suddenly burst forth from a neighbouring post. Leaving the other sentry to keep watch, I went along to investigate. Flames were issuing from a dug-out, whose sides, revetted with brushwood, were burning like tinder. The collecting crowd was soon dispersed by an officer who had appeared on the scene. It seemed that the enemy would be bound to shell such a conspicuous target. The flames leapt high, illuminating the area with a reddish glare, while clouds of smoke billowed across the trenches to the rear. But the Austrians took no notice and, except for the crackling of the fire and the unremitting roar of the waters, the night remained calm. Only later did we learn the details of the tragedy. One of the dugout's occupants had accidently kicked over the brazier while still sleeping, and the fire had got a hold so rapidly that one of his colleagues had been caught like a rat in a trap and burned to death. Thus the war of attrition went on, and, wondering who would be next, we took a particularly poor view of possible elimination by such an accident.

On following nights the trenches were a purgatory. All fires in dugouts had been immediately banned, though we would willingly have taken the risk in exchange for even a modest amount of warmth. Whale oil was issued for a daily rubbing of our feet, as a precaution against frost bite. I had not encountered this treatment since the autumn of 1916 when, on the Somme, I had suffered from trench feet and had then formed a poor opinion of the efficacy of this evil-smelling fluid.

On the night of 12 January we left the trenches to take over billets in close support some way above Peneriva. The company was lodged in a large two-storey building of the farm type alongside a road, Number 6 Platoon occupying the upper floor. The Lewis gunners had been assigned to a detached outhouse, alongside a large iron gate, which swung between two massive stone pillars. This single-storey outhouse contained one fairly habitable room abutting the road, and a number of pens or small barns, all in a bad state of repair. We were not sorry to be on our own, but, despite the large fireplace with which our 'living room' was equipped and the relative abundance of fuel, we were still unable to keep really warm, so intense was the cold at that period.

All was quiet in the neighbourhood during the daytime, which we passed pleasantly on aeroplane guard. Movement had to be kept at a minimum, since we were under direct enemy observation. The slopes of the Montello, which began a few hundred yards behind the billet, looked very beautiful in the sunshine, which was again continuous. Batteries, dug in not far away, took an occasional shot at the enemy. Otherwise there was little to suggest that there was a war on. The continual bustle of transports and working parties that had been the normal accompaniment of war on the Western Front, was entirely absent here. Down the road the West Yorkshires had opened a canteen, which was available to all. Their display of good things right in the line took our breath away. Notes of some purchases which I made show the following items and prices paid (expressed in lire, then worth sixpence, a sum which would be many times greater than its modern equivalent):

Small tin of salmon: 2.30
Boot polish: 0.85
Sardines: 2.00
Chocolate (small packet): 2.20
Erasmic soap: 1.00
Collins 9d novel (cloth bound): 3.30

We considered ourselves fortunate, yet on the third night in this pleasant rural retreat there was an incident, normal enough in war, which because of its sudden contrast and grave personal impact, has registered itself deep in my memory.

We had indulged in a carouse around the fire and were endeavouring to woo sleep by keeping out the increasing cold under our blankets, when a gun began to fire away in the far distance. The discharge rang clearly over the night air; the shell moaned over and burst with a low report. One of those small mountain batteries, I thought, dropping its innocuous 'bullets' in our vicinity, nothing really to worry about. A short spell and the shelling ceased. I dozed off.

It must have been about midnight when the battery opened up again. The bursts were nearer this time and, it would seem, not far from the billet. We were getting somewhat jumpy, only our Polish comrade showing no inclination to allow natural fear to overcome natural laziness. Indeed he wanted to be allowed to sleep and was caustic in his comments on fools who had got the wind up. In view of his normal attitudes I found this something of a cheek. To me there was an indefinable sense of menace in the air, a quite irrational sense, exaggerated no doubt by the surrounding quiet. Half-dressed, with Westgarth, who as Number One felt a special responsibility, I went outside to look round. It was a magnificent night. A thousand stars twinkled through the crisp cold air, endowing the surrounding scene with an almost ethereal look. We could discover no shell-holes near the billet, at least within the distance at which we had adjudged shells to have burst, and we returned to bed definitely mystified, if somewhat reassured. I bedded down between the blankets again, in the corner of the room nearest the roadway, which I was sharing with Tom Ireland. All was now unearthly still outside, and my companions were soon snoring.

The minutes passed slowly and I dozed but lightly. Normally I was not apprehensive like this, and had slept through much more obvious dangers in Flanders, when the nightly shelling of rear camps was never unexpected. There must have been some special premonition of danger in my soul that night, abetted no doubt by the intense cold. A further hour wore slowly away. Suddenly that same report came clearly through the still night air. I was wide awake on the instant. The shell was screaming nearer and nearer … I lit our candle. My companions were already bustling up as the missile burst with a loud explosion not far away. The truth now dawned clearly in our minds: this was no light shell, a heavy battery was firing. Our previous perspectives had been all wrong. The entire section were now hurrying into their clothing. Corporal Goffee advised an exit to the short covered trench constructed for such an emergency some thirty yards or so behind the outhouse. Meanwhile the second shell burst with a shattering roar on the road in front; heavy materials thudded against the outside wall and the whole billet rocked, equipments fell from their nails, and candles were extinguished. The third shell was on its way. I had my hand on the door catch, as we all bunched forward ready to leave. 'Wait!' shouted the corporal, and I held the door to while the shell burst directly in front, blasting a shower of stones and shrapnel against the panels. I flung the door wide and we rushed into the night with the sound of the last discharge in our ears. The last missile was on its way and the battery was about to achieve its target. Even as we threw ourselves through the trench-opening, there was a rending explosion behind us, while a rain of bricks and muck fell all around. We knew, before our eyes bore witness to the fact, that the billet had been destroyed. That was the battery's last shoot that night, and it was quite fortuitous that the direct hit should have been made by the last shot of all. Or was it?

When a little later we ventured back we found the outhouse smashed in like an egg, though we could see little else in the gloom that now lay about us. We blundered into Sergeant-Major Rhodes, who had come out to investigate and was flashing his hand-torch over the pile of rubble. 'Good God,' he exclaimed, in a voice charged with emotion and relief, 'I never expected to see any of you alive'.

Shortly after daybreak we went along hopefully to salvage our kits. What a sight met our eyes! The last shell had burst in the corner where Tom and I had been lying. The neighbouring walls were shattered and our belongings, buried under a heap of bricks and plaster, were smashed to pulp. The chimney stack, laid bare through the gaping roof, was decorated with shreds of equipment and personal kit like a grotesque Christmas tree. Even the ground sheets and blankets, spread on the floor, were riddled with holes. The far sides of the room were not so badly damaged but there remained not a square foot of floor, wall or ceiling unmarked by shrapnel, and it seemed almost certain that no member of the section would have survived. Of the fate of Tom and I there could have been no room for doubt.

The incident was thoroughly investigated and the general conclusion was that the shells had come from a mobile heavy gun of about 8-inch calibre, probably brought forward on the railway for a special shoot. I kept a fragment of the shrapnel as a souvenir. No doubt the enemy gunners were searching for one of our hidden batteries. The missiles must have hurtled over the main billet, which they may have imagined was masking the gun. If so their marksmanship was particularly impressive. The second shell seems to have fallen just in front of the massive gate-post abutting the outhouse, to which it had acted as a sort of shield, for the pillar had been lifted bodily into the air, breaking into large chunks. Had this not been there the last shell would have found its task already accomplished.

Much of that day I spent in an attempt to salvage my kit, but there was little to be retrieved. Even my rifle was a travesty of twisted metal, only a small round brass plate from the butt remaining as a complete part. A collection of post cards of places we had passed through were scattered over the field on the far side of the road, tattered and torn of course; while my wallet, containing photographs and letters, was picked up some way down the road. All that remained were the contents of my pockets, my steel helmet and the box respirator, which I was wearing.

Everything had to be reported in detail and there was some talk of a court martial by one of the officers, who may have been joking. Loss of rifle and kit while on active service — and we were officially in the line — was a military crime, punishable by a long term in the glasshouse. It is difficult today to believe that any such issue could have been raised in the particular circumstances, but one could not be too sure, such were the different attitudes of those days, when pre-war ideas of strict soldierly conduct enshrined in King's Regulations continued to have sway. Be all that as it may, I have it on record that Sergeant-Major Rhodes, who was certainly not the emotional type, considered the suggestion sufficiently serious to declare publicly that such talk was nonsense and that the company was fortunate not to have to make up for the loss of an efficient Lewis gun section. This was plain speaking for those days, even from one of warrant rank, for the slightest public criticism, even by implication, of members of the officer class, was regarded almost as blasphemy. Only the rankers could afford to speak their minds, with the usual larding of four-letter expletives.

When we withdrew a few days later to the old billets in Biadene, I carried my few belongings in a sandbag and was sufficiently military-minded not to like my unsoldierly distinction when marching in the ranks. I had to await new equipment from stores and, incidentally, there was no monetary compensation to purchase certain personal small kit which was necessary. In view of my ill-equipped state I was placed on mess orderly duties, a menial job which had certain advantages. Thus, I missed the usual preliminary agonies of the full-scale inspection carried out on 26 January by the brigadier-general.

The company was in the mood to relax. On the previous Sunday, when church and pay parades coincided, there had been celebrations and a general row in the billets afterwards. I do not remember what it was all about, and probably did not know at the time. These occasions just arose. Drink releases pent-up passions and, as we had experienced in France, murder could have occurred at such times. On this particular occasion a number of NCOs were 'put on the peg'. Our platoon sergeant, an amiable soul, had a show on his own. He pushed his fist through the glass panel of one of the billet doors, in mistake for a pal's physiognomy. The following day he was going about with his arm swathed in bandages, in mortal fear of too-close an inquiry into his 'accident', which, I am sure, took no one in. The company was much amused.

The following week the same routine was followed, and I joined the revellers in Montebelluna, but not to drink. There was the recently opened YMCA to visit and a picture show in the divisional theatre. I wish I had kept a note of the films projected on that occasion, but I have not the least recollection of what they were. There were probably a number of shorts, and it would not be surprising if one of the Keystone Chaplins was included. Whatever they were, the novelty of a film show so far from home would have ensured maximum enjoyment on the audience's part.

Warnings on the potency of the local *vino rosso* had gone unheeded, and the wine shops were reaping a rich harvest in lire. That same night there followed another fracas in the billet. At least half the company had rolled home drunk. Unfortunately this included the Lewis gun section, except for Tom and me, who had opted out. Corporal Goffee, old campaigner as he was, had found no difficulty in drinking the others under the table. Under his leadership as host for the occasion they had gone with the fixed intention of having a booze-up. The results must have exceeded their expectations. During the night most of our companions were as sick as dogs, and the following morning our room was in an indescribable state. With the fetid atmosphere of the small room, our blankets soiled or threatened on all sides by the expelled half-consumed wine, my companions white-faced and groaning with internal discomfort, I thought when I awoke from a fitful slumber that I had landed in some special section of Dante's Inferno. To throw open doors and windows wide, to fling on one's clothes, and to flee into the open air was an immediate necessity to avoid joining the repentant revellers in their particular revulsions. At that moment it was not easy to avoid a feeling of self-righteousness at this picture of normal gentle men driven by hopeless, deadly monotony to seek diversion at the price of becoming like senseless beasts, wallowing in their own filth. In retrospective extenuation, I can write that this particular group did not frequently indulge themselves in this way, nor do I recollect that they ever showed resentment to those of us who chose to enjoy ourselves in our own way.

On the morning after — it was Monday 28 January — excitement came to the village. The sun was shining, as only the Italian sun can shine in January, lighting up the snow-capped mountain peaks clearly against a sky of softly graded blueness. Over the countryside peace presided, with the distant farmhouses of the Montello basking in a slumberous loveliness. Green fields with white buildings speckling the landscape, the narrow stream on the far side of the road welling noiselessly with cool crystal water straight from the mountains, the street almost deserted at that hour — all this I could see from the billet window, as I plodded slowly through a lesson of Hugo's Italian course. Suddenly a whistle blew and a droning became audible in the sky.

The machine, a large Austrian scout plane, came into view as if from nowhere, and our placid landscape was transformed into a ring of belching fire. Anti-aircraft shells screamed up, bursting in white puffs above the valley. Machine guns rattled from the street below, some even being fired from windows of the billets. The enemy plane swooped and twisted, attempting to evade the fire. Then two Italian planes appeared from across the hills behind us and gave chase. The fire from the ground became intermittent, ceasing each time an Allied machine came near the line of fire. Yet it seemed a miracle that they were not hit by the friendly batteries. The three machines now seemed to be manoeuvring barely higher than the top of the Montello, over which the enemy plane needed to escape. They seemed as though they were staging a special stunt for us as audience within the arena of hills, but of course it was all in deadly earnest and we watched spellbound. The pursued tried desperately to escape, dodging backwards and forwards with great skill, as the two Italian aviators closed in upon him. At each approach the combatants fired their machine guns until they passed out of range. It was a breathless encounter, followed excitedly by hundreds of watchers from the street below and from the surrounding houses. The odds were too much against the enemy. The Italian machines manoeuvred to and fro, performing miracles of clever turning, backing and diving hither and thither, as they relentlessly edged their quarry towards the hillside. The fight ended as suddenly as it had begun. Darting away from his pursuers, the Austrian found himself enveloped by the barrage. Something happened: the machine seemed to lose life; it slipped through the air without volition to crash in a heap on the bank of the Montello. A mighty cheer arose for the victors, who disappeared as quickly as they had come. The guns ceased and, but for the knots of hurrying figures making across the fields towards the distant wreckage, all signs of conflict melted back into the previous calm, while the sun continued to shine down, heedless of the petty struggles of humanity. We had witnessed a fight to the death, which left in my mind a clear-cut picture that would last for many a long day, a trivial incident in that vast conflict, which, because of its spectacular nature, was bound to survive many more important happenings. It is a sad recollection that few of the witnesses — and this included myself at the time — were likely to have given sympathetic thought to the young life, thus cut short, and of his bereaved relations at home in Austria, who would never know what had happened to him.

A few days later my new equipment was issued from the stores, and I was doubly glad both to lose my uniqueness and to be relieved from dish-scouring and ministering to the grousing, not very grateful, platoon. In the army all the faults to be expected from communist living are plainly manifested.

We left for the line again that evening, 3 February. Despite the clearness of the night and the quiescence of the enemy, my nerves were in a particularly jumpy state. The picture of that shattered billet remained clearly in my mind, while my ears were for ever on the *qui vive* for that distant gun's discharge. It was all so silly, yet so real at the time. The very quietness helped to prevent one's courage from being suitably keyed to the occasion. Yet the rest of the platoon were also decidedly jumpy, so that my own peculiar state was obviously not entirely attributable to the particular incident. We seemed more nervy than we had appeared normally to be when entering the dreaded Salient. Nothing happened that night. No better proof could be imagined of Shakespeare's dictum about the many deaths of cowards!

We were holding a position on the right brigade front, the Lewis gun teams of both Number 5 and 6 Platoons being attached to 'C' Company in close support. We shared a large dugout in the Montello hillside, with its entrance debouching into a grassy gully, worn down by the rains and running at right angles to the line. A trench out of the gully led round to the front of the hill, where our excellently sited gun-post commanded a wide expanse of river.

Instructions having been issued that we should tidy up the trench, we pottered about with pick and shovel, killing time and trying to look busy whenever strangers came in sight. But there was plenty of time for 'chatting', and reading and hobnobbing with the other section, whose members were known to us by sight. At the upper end of the gully the trench came into view by way of a steep stairway. We were thus able to detect in good time the occasional approach of parties of officers, who almost invariably found something about our domestic arrangements to criticise, although they were not altogether consistent in their admonitions.

Daytime turns on sentry were a delight to me. Over the wide riverbed numerous turbulent greenish-blue streaks of water, rippling with white foam, streamed away to the east, while the vast mountain wall towered in serene magnificence on the far side. Immediately beyond the river the countryside, with its criss-crossing roads and numerous buildings, spread out before us like some immense map with only the names missing. I never tired of the miracle of that view, which was incomparably more wonderful than any scene that I had hitherto gazed upon.

In retrospect I recognise two personalities in the other team who impressed themselves upon my consciousness: one a slightly-built quiet senior gunner who, when I next saw him some months later, lay sprawled beside me with his life's blood draining rapidly away; the other a fine strapping fellow, only temporarily attached to the team, whom we knew very well because, on account of his fine figure and smart military bearing, he was frequently chosen for battalion ceremonial guard. I will call him K, as it would not be fair to place his name on record. At this time he was in a bad state of nerves. This we soon gathered from the constant leg-pulling and baiting of his companions, who were using him as a means of release for their own less apparent misgivings.

One afternoon I shared the sentry turn with K, who was quite a pleasant fellow. Our artillery had been active for some time, and we were all fed up with what we considered to be a quite unnecessary stirring up of trouble. Already the other section, simulating wind up in an advanced stage, had sown the idea in my companion's head that this military preparation was the prelude to an enemy attack. Since the enemy was not even deigning to reply, this was a notion too absurd even to need refutation. The shells screaming over from behind us were in the main falling on a large island out in the riverbed, where they seemed to be bursting near what looked like trench works. The shooting seemed to be pretty good, but it was a pity, I thought, thus to spoil the serene grandeur of that lovely scene.

My companion was in a pathetic condition. I was reassuring. After all the enemy was doing nothing, but he considered that in itself highly suspicious. I did not participate in the leg-pulling, largely because I knew only too well what it was like to be really frightened and could see nothing funny in others showing similar symptoms. Some of K's companions strolled up to the post to add fuel to the fire. News had come, they averred, that the Austrians were planning to attack at nightfall, and our artillery, by shelling the assembly points, was attempting to forestall the enemy's plan. They embroidered this tale with numerous circumstantial details, winking at me behind the victim's back. Never did I see anyone in such a state with such little cause. K was shaking like a leaf, his nervousness having banished all reason. I laughed with the rest, feeling that if he could be so gullible he deserved little sympathy, but there was a wry element in my mirth. However, I doubt whether this silly and unimportant incident would have been brought so clearly to my mind, had not K been awarded a Military Medal in our last great battle. It was to be maliciously said then that K's prowess on headquarters guard had helped to put him in the picture, which could very well have been true, without detracting from his worthiness on the occasion.

Actually the only other significant happening during this uneventful trench tour was the departure of some of the battalion on home leave. We envied them but were glad, for every such departure shortened the waiting list. On the night of 10 February we were withdrawn to reserve billets at Volpago, situated behind the Montello, away to the right. During the next day or two we assisted the Royal Engineers in making a road over the hill. We were at this time introduced to our new medical officer, who held one of those routine inspections to which we were so accustomed. He was an American who had so effectively acquired our own medical officers' methods as to beat them at their own game, by creating the impression that he was dealing with a pack of slackers and lead-swingers to whom the merest fraction of an inch would be taken as a mile. Naturally we resented this even more from a foreigner.

One day we carried out battalion manoeuvres in a heavy snowstorm, which showed how changeable the weather conditions could be at that time and place. Captain Stirling went on the warpath over the loss of cap-badges and jack-knives, which were both in great demand among the Italians. Penalties were exacted and everyone was getting into very bad humour over it all. The captain seemed to delight in taking it out of us, and was not going the right way about making himself popular with his comparatively new command.[4] We were all pleased therefore when we marched rearwards from Volpago on 17 February and found ourselves billeted in a large second-floor loft of a farm building in a small village, some eleven miles from Montebelluna. The name of the place I did not record and have been unable to identify, but there were a number of factors at the time that helped to register our stay there in my memory.

Not that there was anything memorable about the place, which was just another village with few diversions. The billet was comfortable enough, the loft being sufficiently roomy to house the entire company without crowding. Wooden beams under the roof afforded admirable facilities for hanging our equipment. They interlaced with roof supports at intervals, conveniently dividing the floor space into compartments. At night the place was a forest of rifles, equipment, mess tins and the rest, suspended from wires and beams above our heads. It was to be expected that the orderly officer would have all this altered in the daytime, when our kit had to be arranged on the floor in strict regulation order.

We soon began to lose our rations, and discovered that the place was infested with rats, large well-fed agile beasts with

---

[4] He had taken over command of the company after the death of Captain West in the Menin Road attack on 20 September 1917.

high circus qualifications. They performed — dark moving shadows — on the beams above our heads at night. On the very first night I was awakened by a large brute that had leapt upon my chest on his way to some appointment. We were not too bothered about all this, since rats were not uncommon visitors in the trenches, but we took a poor view over the theft of our food. One evening, as I sat quietly in the billet writing a letter, a dark furry form slithered silently down the wire, at the end of which my mess tin was suspended. This regular Blondin of a rat cleared off before my eyes with a slice of bread in his jaws. A more secure larder had to be discovered, but nothing edible could go into one's pack. A member of the platoon had a hole gnawed into his while asleep, the thief having successfully tracked down a succulent piece of cheese.

Enemy aircraft were getting more active in these back areas during the night. Consequently we had the job of sandbagging hutments and tents at a nearby military aerodrome. With improving weather this was quite pleasant work. The Flying Corps NCOs, under whom we were working, told us that greater activities were to be expected shortly on the front, and this was why the defence works were being pressed forward. When they heard that we were Lewis gunners they suggested that we should seek transfers to them, since machine gunners were in great demand. True, it was a hazardous job, but there was always a comfortable billet to come back to, and frequent leave home. Sergeants' stripes would be granted straight away and there would be a course of instruction in England. To home-starved infantrymen this sounded very attractive, and I was among those who put in applications for transfer through the company office.

Towards the end of the week there was a pay parade, followed by drink and the usual ructions in the billet — free fights and filth. Our release from the tensions of the Salient was clearly not improving our morale, nor was it easy to keep clear of the troubles with so many of us cooped up together. The following night a woman came into the billet downstairs, a country-woman, but whether she was young or old I do not know. The news spread quickly and men, of whom I had a better opinion, disappeared in ones and twos to the lower storey, returning later with looks of sly elation tinged with shame as of schoolboys who had just robbed an orchard. Then they began to describe the affair, first by innuendo but soon, as they gained confidence with increasing numbers, more boldly. I was confused with shame and wanted to stop up my ears. I wanted to get away, but dared not leave the billet lest I be included with the rest. The woman, it appeared, who had been seen loitering about the area, had wandered into the lower billet, which was unoccupied. She had been seen by one of the men, who attempted to embrace her — the story he told himself — and she had resisted. In the scuffle they had fallen to the ground. Then others had appeared on the scene and men had become lustful beasts struggling over her prostrate body. These things I pieced together from the general pattern of the affair, which went on for some time.

It was perhaps as well that the next morning we were ordered back to the line. The order had come out of the blue. The urgency of the call was indicated by the fact that lorries were sent to take us back to Biadene. It was the old Biadene but with a difference. On the opposite side of the road a Soldier's Home had been fitted out, though at the moment there was nothing for sale. There were many more, and larger, shell holes in the vicinity, and soon after our arrival a heavy shell fell in the village some couple of hundred yards away.

Our first idea was that an attack was being launched across the river, but rumour soon provided the report — which was to prove correct — that the division in the line had been ordered back to France. For once we were not sorry to be the relieving force, and the West Kents, whom we replaced on the right flank of the left-brigade front at the river's edge, were not pleased to see us. They had already been told of their destination.

While our destinies were being decided in the conclaves of the powerful — not, as history was to record, without a good deal of somewhat childish quarrelling — our days on the Montello Front, which were running out much faster than we realised at the time, were characterised by the normal routines.

Not that the battle line was quite so quiet as it had been. The enemy guns were more active. Shells came over now and again, bursting near the trench and filling the air with flying stones. This was a novel experience for us on this front, and it was plain that the fortifications of the riverbank would make a poor showing under serious bombardment. At night we could watch enemy battery flashes lighting up hollows in the hillside, which our guns then attempted to locate, not very successfully as far as we could see.

The captain and the sergeant-major took a personal interest in pressing forward with trench duties and working parties. With our nights broken as a result of the continuous sentry duties, we usually counted upon snatching forty winks at some time during the day, but something had spurred headquarters into action and no one was allowed a moment's peace. Those of us who had shown interest in the Flying Corps transfer were informed by the captain that we would be expected to sign on for at least three years, to which we answered unanimously that we were not prepared to serve a day longer than was necessary.

Although the war seemed likely to go on endlessly we still could not conceive of its lasting for another three years.

On 28 February our small cloth PH helmets, which we had continued to carry in addition to the much more effective box respirator, were at last collected into store, and we welcomed the loss of an item of equipment that had long ceased to be anything more than an encumbrance. The authorities had taken time enough to make up their minds.

Following a spell of bright fine weather, there was now a great change. Heavy rain-laden clouds lowered down from the mountains, turning the sparkling green of the waters to a turbid gray. For more than twenty-four hours the scene was changing as though in preparation for a really dirty spell. Then, on the second evening, it began to drizzle and all our usual landmarks were blotted out. This was but a prelude. During the night of 1 March the storm broke in earnest, swamping us out. Our flimsy shelters were no match for the waters, which washed loose rubble into the trench and drenched us in no time. The Piave began to rise; the roar of the waters became deafening. Our patrols barely managed to withdraw in time, and an advance post had only just recrossed from mid-stream when the only footbridge collapsed and whirled away seawards. The turbulent waters, rushing ever and ever more widely over the shingle, threw up waves of white foam wherever they passed over some submerged object. All sorts of debris came down from the mountains: uprooted trees and riven branches, boxes, furniture, lumps of wood. A tin box, chattering over the stones, was used as a target from the trenches. Smaller streams coalesced into wide torrents, the nearest of which lapped the bank not more than fifteen yards from our position, which nevertheless stood high enough to be safe for the time being.

On the following day the waters were still rising, the islands were shrinking fast and the Piave had become a mighty expanse of water dividing us absolutely from the enemy. We were soaked to the skin and had given up all idea of trying to get dry, but the position was still tenable. The Austrians were not faring so well. Over on the plain, situated half-right from where we were, a hectic withdrawal was obviously taking place. Though it was too far away for us to see the evacuation with the naked eye, our artillery, harassing the enemy's movements, indicated clearly what was happening. We watched the guns registering on different targets and counted the shots required to blow up some white-faced building with a direct hit, as a cloud of brick and plaster shot into the air. We had no pity for those sufferers on the far side, and even regarded this demonstration as a welcome interest to distract our minds from our own discomforts. At any moment the Austrians might decide to give tit for tat, as the Germans certainly would have done, but nothing of this sort happened. Possibly their gunners were themselves too personally involved to retaliate, though there were batteries on high ground which certainly could have made us uncomfortable.

On 4 March the storm began to abate and by the time we were relieved from our uncomfortable position on the following evening it was fine again. Yet, as we were passing through a village just behind the trenches, a brilliant glare suddenly seemed to originate in the air above us, causing us to scatter wildly in all directions towards the walls of the square which we were crossing. These walls were lit up momentarily as if by the light of day, and there was really something unearthly about this awesome flash, which, for a terrorising moment, we took for the bursting of a large shell that had arrived unheralded in the heavens above us. Then there was a tremendous thunderclap, as a torrential sheet of water enveloped us out of the skies. The rains of the preceding days were immediately eclipsed by this sudden deluge. It was difficult to run for shelter: the rain splashed up in waves from the ground, as though the river itself had risen and was engulfing us. Movement was impeded, breathing almost impossible. Despite my waterproof and heavy topcoat I felt the cold water flowing over my skin and thought I was back in the icy stream again. It was all over in a few moments. The downpour cleared as quickly as it had come and the tempest began to give way to a starry sky. We looked upon each other's dripping forms with amazement, spellbound at experiencing so much rain in so short a time, and only slowly realising that we had been involved in a spectacular cloudburst. As we marched away under a wonderous tapestry of stars the rain literally drained out of us.

Our billet at Pederiva — a large store-room on the second floor — was the very acme of comfort after our recent experiences. During the next few days we had plenty to do in restoring our sodden equipment to some semblance of smartness. On the second morning there was an incident that caused much amusement. The officers were occupying a room below us and one, who was not particularly popular, had some suspicious moisture drop upon his bed during the night. He appeared in the billet in a towering rage and interrogated everyone in the approximate vicinity of the spot where the moisture must have gone through the ceiling below. Now it was the custom of some to use their boots at night as illicit containers, in preference to traipsing downstairs out into the yard, and it was always possible for a full boot to be kicked over. Of course by the time the investigator appeared on the scene all boots were being properly worn. Whether or not he knew of the particular custom, there was no evidence to support his well-justified suspicions. The men were extremely polite and helpful. 'No doubt the rain had dripped through.' 'We came in very wet you know, sir.' The officer was nonplussed. Still fuming and uttering dire threats should this happen again, he retreated, leaving the platoon to enjoy the joke.

After a few days, during which I was pleased to be measured by the regimental tailors for a new tunic, we switched over to the very billet from which the section had been shelled, but now we found a place in the main building. The loveliest spring was beginning to permeate the surrounding countryside. About this time I read of the sinking of the *Glenart Castle*, the hospital ship in which I had been taken to Blighty at Christmas time in 1916. In this vast impersonal conflict it was such comparatively unimportant incidents, with which one had happened to have personal associations, that impressed themselves upon one's memory.

On 12 March we were ordered to clean up the billets. By teatime we had everything shipshape and our kit ready to move off. The Italians were taking over from us. Our spell on the Montello front was ending. We were light of heart. Even though things had not been at all bad here, any sort of change was to be welcomed. In the early evening we sat round a brazier singing with gusto, if not always in tune, the old songs which have continued for another half century to impress themselves upon successive generations. The sing-song was abruptly terminated by a request for working parties to go to headquarters to bring out the usual clobber. No doubt movements along the front had made the enemy uneasy, for now they began to shell the Montello slopes a little way back from the billet. They were obviously searching for one of our batteries that had been firing during the day. The artillerymen's shelter caught fire, but they managed to keep the flames away from the stacked ammunition. Shells began to drop along the road and to pepper the area round the billet. Fortunately these shells were of extremely light calibre and did little harm. But they burst venomously in the gathering dusk and we began to wonder whether we had been counting our chickens. We were getting into a state of nerves not unusual on such occasions, and were not sorry to see the arrival of a column of drab figures, moving in under the burden of hefty packs, which they were obviously glad to throw off. The newcomers seemed subdued and different from the light-hearted Italians whom we had previously encountered. Yet the shelling, which was still continuing in a desultory sort of way, did not seem to affect them in the least. I was quite amazed at their sang-froid, which I could not help contrasting with my own feelings at the moment.

After stopping for the night in Biadene, we marched on the following day twenty miles under a sweltering sun back to Castelfranco, which we reached in early afternoon. At the bottom of a little green field behind our billet, in an empty house just outside the town, ran a cool stream, in whose limpid waters it was heavenly to bathe our feet, and to laze on the grassy bank, with visions of a period of rest ahead of us.

HISTORICAL NOTE: SPRING REORGANISATION

Proposals to reduce the strength of the Italian Expeditionary Force and to reinforce the Western Front with the withdrawn troops had first been considered as recently as 15 February. There had indeed been previous discussion of a plan to add Italian divisions to the armies in France, and Sir Douglas Haig was now asked whether he would prefer to be reinforced by two British or by four Italian divisions from the Italian front. He chose the former alternative. On the evening of 22 February General Plumer issued orders that the 41st and 7th Divisions should proceed to France as soon as possible. All this was very quick work, and as the 23rd Division's orders to relieve units of the 41st Division were received only two days later, no further explanation is needed of our surprise at the 11th Northumberland's sudden move at that time. The Italians were certainly justified in their annoyance at thus being faced by a *fait accompli*.

The 41st Division detrained in France between 6 and 13 March, but in the meantime transfer of the 7th Division had been held up pending formal consultation through the Executive Committee at Versailles, a step that had previously been omitted. Some of their advance troops were already on the train when the move was suspended. The net result of all this was that the 5th Division was substituted for the 7th, the latter remaining with us on the Italian front until the end of the campaign. The entrainment of the 5th Division began on 1 April.

Before this, on 10 March, Lord Cavan had taken over command of the British forces in Italy from General Plumer, who was to return to France. It is in no way to detract from the distinguished record of our new leader in his new command to state that by this change the British on the Italian Front had lost, not only one of the outstanding leaders of the First World War, but one whose great popularity with the troops was rooted in their feeling that this strict old aristocrat had a genuine sympathy for the men in the ranks, on whom people in his position had so often to call to perform the impossible.

By the end of March three of the six French divisions had been withdrawn from Italy, General Maistre having been replaced by General Graziani (a Frenchman despite his Italian name). This meant that the British and French each had three divisions remaining in Italy. At the same time the Italians had agreed to send their 3rd and 8th Divisions as a token force to the French front.

5: CHANGE OF FRONT

On the following day we marched back a further thirty kilometres, through ancient Cittadella, to the little village of Quinto, not far from Vicenza. The weather had turned cooler, otherwise the march would have been trying beyond measure. Our new billets were a row of straggling farm buildings situated down a short side lane, which petered out in the fields. Some of us were assigned to an open loft above a cowshed, with which at the outset we were not very impressed. We had to mount to our sleeping place by a ladder and climb on the top of deep layers of fresh hay. In fact, this bed was most comfortable and there was the added advantage of sleeping in the fresh air. We woke in the morning feeling on top of the world.

The brief interlude at Quinto was enjoyable, despite the usual annoyances of army routine, which were always accentuated as soon as we got away from the grim business of the trenches. The weather was wonderful, like warm summer days in England. We were able to supplement our rations with eggs and milk. The former were 25 *centissimi* each and the milk, which came steaming from the cows, milked by the girls morning and evening in the shed below, was 50 *centissimi* a pint. We had no qualms about tuberculosis bacilli!

We had our parades and undertook route marches through the surrounding countryside, whose marvellous irrigation constantly amazed me. There was a mimic attack on the village, in which the various 'sides' got mixed up and the company officers came under a good deal of criticism from their seniors for the results. There was the discovery in a neighbouring village of an army canteen with ample stores of biscuits and chocolate, and there was a compulsory parade to watch our platoon play Number 7 at soccer, the match ending in a draw. Compulsory sport was extremely unpopular even with addicts, of whom we had plenty, for the company's sporting record was an excellent one, but this was the only time that I experienced anything of this sort in the army. No doubt the imposition on this occasion was the outcome of someone's bad temper: possibly Captain Stirling's, who still made little effort to hide his lukewarmness for his company.

At this time the red, white and blue ribbon of the 1914-15 Star (a more generalised version of the Mons Star, which had been rightly reserved for the Old Contemptibles, who had actually taken part in the famous retreat from Mons) was issued to all troops who had gone overseas before 1916. Most of the ribbons in our company went to the recent transferees from non-infantry branches, who were naturally very proud of their distinction. While envying them their medal we felt that service in the supply and technical corps was of small merit compared with infantry service, though they themselves had, as yet, experienced little to enable them to appreciate our point of view. It was at this same period that the active service chevrons appeared. These were diminutive inverted chevrons to be worn on the lower part of the right sleeve of the tunic: a red chevron for 1914 and a blue one for other years, each man being entitled to the first on coming abroad and one additional chevron on completion of each full year of active service. These were of little significance until one went home, when they served to distinguish the active-service from the home-service soldier. At one of the weekly pay parades about this time we all agreed to allocate one day's pay to the Northumberland Prisoners' Fund, an organisation set up to provide comforts through the Red Cross to prisoners of war in enemy hands.

One day we were taken out to practice with the Yukon pack, some examples of which had been dug out of store. We remembered the occasion in the Salient when similar exercises had foreshadowed the use of this carrying contraption for increasing mobility over the mud of Passchendaele. Now, as on the previous occasion, nothing further was to materialise, but we gathered at the time that the pack's possibilities were being explored because of our imminent transfer to a new front.

During our brief stay at this farm — or small-holding would perhaps be a more appropriate term — I had an idyllic experience unique in my army service. With the Italian peasants in our billet, who were poor and hard-working as only such workers can be, we had quickly established good relations, and I personally, as one of the few with some small knowledge of their language, soon found them very friendly. There were two young girls in their early teens, a middle-aged woman, an old woman, and two men of doubtful age, who appeared only occasionally on the scene. This was the normal pattern of the Italian household at the time: all the able-bodied men were away and those who remained seemed to be busy from morning to night.

The two girls were attractive but perhaps too young to draw upon themselves the usual attention of the foreign soldiery. They were certainly well conducted and invariably went down to the bottom of the field together, an excursion occasionally necessary to all members of the household in the absence of normal sanitary contrivances in the house! Although the parlour was scantily furnished and showed every sign of poverty, the whole place was kept spotlessly clean. When the women were not scrubbing or using the broom they would be sewing or undertaking some service for the animals.

At this time one of the cows in the stall below us was about to calve, a matter of very great importance to the household. During the last day or two a continuous vigil was maintained by one of the girls and it was during this time that my personal relationships with them became very close. They would sit and sew in the stall itself and perhaps play cards, delighting to show me their game and to exchange words in the two languages. Without thought or design I found myself becoming fond of the elder girl and was somewhat flattered by an apparent competition between the two of them for my interest. I came to begrudge the time when other activities kept me away from the billet and almost to forget the distant image of the boyhood sweetheart, who, throughout these anxious years, had acted as a sort of protectress of a boy whose romantic heart otherwise hardly wavered, sometimes under the sorest temptation. This was indeed her ultimate office, for the romantic dreams woven round her personality were never to become reality. During these happy days at Quinto that unsubstantial dream came nearer to shattering than at any other time. My heart was filled with a longing not to be understood in terms of the carnal realities of normal army relationships, which had always filled me with aversion.

One evening when a number of us were gathered before the billet I was suddenly jolted by a jocular reference to my interest in the young Italians. It was a shock to realise that my growing infatuation was being noticed but, looking back, I can see how obvious this must have been to all my companions, who, knowing my normal attitudes, must have been genuinely though sympathetically amused at what was happening. But there were two members of the party who were far from sympathetic. At twenty, I was probably the youngest member of the platoon, at a period when company age levels were at their highest. The two critical ones were both in my own age group, and as soon as their accusatory remarks were superimposed upon the general conversation, I recognised in them a fierce rivalry, which was accentuated by the fact that normally we were all such very good friends. The tone of their remarks shocked me and filled me with indignation, but did not have the effect of driving me back into my shell. Indeed, I voiced my resentment at their insinuations in no unmeasured terms. I felt that we were near to blows that would have been delivered in deepest hate, but the threatened battle did not take place. Possibly some degree of support for me among the less interested audience had an influence on my critics.

My eyes had been opened. Now I was a self-appointed Galahad to protect these girls against the sexual designs of my rivals. But I was already established on such a footing of friendship that the threat to my protégées' virtue could have been only a very distant one and I do not think it developed very seriously except in my own mind.

One night there were many animal cries from the stalls below us and much coming and going from outside; and in the morning the household were rejoicing at the safe appearance of a healthy young calf. Opportunity for closer tête-à-têtes and the impulse to kiss my Italian enchantress, which I had been too shy to follow, were now removed, and I could see her only in the parlour with all the others. Yet I felt that we had an understanding and was distracted at heart by the impossible barrier that our situation seemed to place between us. What would have happened had our stay at Quinto been longer I do not know, for I was emotionally much involved at the time. Today I can look back over the years and wonder what happened to my little *signorina*. Did she ever give this unknown foreigner from the cold north another thought? Her destiny as an Italian peasant woman could not have been enviable, for in the sunny south the women, so blooming in their early youth, soon become old and worn through work and the elements, as well as the small reason they have for keeping themselves attractive. She had to survive the dangers of that first war, the rigours of the inter-war years, and the even worse perils of a second war. Yet she may still be alive, the honoured grandmother of many young Italians, oblivious of the fact that she left in the memory of an English soldier, who passed her way for but a few days, an idyllically happy memory when so much else has been forgotten.

It was on 23 March when the rumour that we were going to the mountains first gained currency, just two days before our actual departure, although the Yukon pack incident should have raised our suspicions. The Allied leaders had been expecting a counter-blow from the enemy. It had to fall before the balance of military power finally swung in the Allies' favour. In consequence strategic plans for the Italian Front were tentative, and suggested counter-thrusts were of a limited nature. The decision, however, had been reached to transfer the British divisions to the mountain-front, and this was to be our immediate destination. The halt at Quinto was merely a step preliminary to our movement northwards to the new front.

At daybreak on 25 March we arose from our warm hay for the last time and made ready to move off at 8.00 am. We were all genuinely sorry to depart. It had been a pleasant break amongst those smiling fields with sufficient food and abundant sunshine. Never before had the company looked so fit as when it lined up in front of our erstwhile billets. Our Italian friends, who had been so kind, assembled to wish us god-speed and for once our departure had the additional wrench of personal parting to add poignancy to the hour. It was like going off to the wars afresh. We were leaving for the war area again and we could see no respite; the thundering guns in France had as yet no special message for our ears. All we could discern was a monotonous future of in-and-out, mapped out ahead into an endless ebb and flow of similar excursions. Our friends waved us off with eyes not dry, but minds no doubt surprised at the offhand, unemotional, way in which we left them. But the outward attitude belied the heavy hearts of many that obeyed the sharp military command to march, and at least one heart was full to overflowing, as for the last time its owner sought with shy indecision the eye of the young *signorina* he was leaving behind.

And so we filed across the fields on to the white road once more. All day we marched, halting for an hour and a half at midday. The sun shone down and the white dust slowly crept upwards from our boots, until at length we came to look like a band of millers. The only out-of-the-ordinary incident which I still remember was our passing an Italian military band in full blast, whose instruments and brash music seemed so different from our own. Later in the afternoon the first green spurs of the Alpine foothills began to push out towards the weary foot-sore column, while the distant skies displayed the line of white-capped peaks of the higher ranges beyond. We reached the small town of Thiene in time for tea, having covered about twenty miles under difficult conditions. Our billet there was a disused factory.

A refreshing draught of tea, followed by vigorous brushings and polishings made expert by continual practice, soon reconverted the millers into soldiers. We were ready to explore our new surroundings, and I remember that my companion on this occasion was Isaac Doniger, with whom acquaintance was rapidly burgeoning into real friendship. Our search was for postcards. Thiene itself was undistinguished; its shops had little for sale. But its strategic position amidst the foothills on a main route into the Alps, barrier against the north, had established its importance since the days of Rome, and its surroundings were magnificent, enhanced for us by the fact that we had hitherto seen the mountains only from afar. Here we were at the very gateway to the heights, and we found ourselves speculating about the routes which led out of town, and wondering which of these would take us up into the fastnesses on the morrow.

While returning along the main street we noticed a queue of Tommies at an undistinguished doorway on the opposite side of the road. An Italian policeman regulated the crowd, which jostled eagerly to enter. It was not a café and I wondered whether it might be a cinema, but there were no announcements of any sort. A passing soldier said it was a red lamp, though at the time we were too incredulous to believe him. It was so manifestly absurd to suggest that a jostling queue of soldiers were openly entering a brothel that we dismissed the incident. It was not until the company began to trickle back into the billet later in the evening that we learned the truth. They recounted with open bravado their adventures in the house of ill-fame, for such it was, and told of unprintable things. Raucous laughter filled the billet and men whom I had always considered decent appeared as brutes. I was nauseated by this reduction to sheer animality of a relationship which I felt could be hallowed only by love, and I found it difficult to avoid being sick. All seemed so sordid and pitiful. But my physical reaction was probably to no small extent due to the cumulative sexual stench which hung about the billet until the next morning. I was glad when, after clearing up the garbage of the night's stay, we marched off at the early hour of 6.00 am.

We struggled forward with two blankets and a jerkin strapped upon our normal load, and wondered why this penance was being imposed; for as usual our future plans had not been disclosed. It was only when we reached an Italian car park about a kilometre outside the town that we discovered that we were to be transported into the mountains. The small but powerful Fiat vans made good headway along the hilly roads and we soon found ourselves mounting well above the foothills into the real mountain regions beyond. The road went up past green fields and little nestling hamlets, turned sharp corners and continued to zigzag skywards, doubling backwards and forwards and drawing us higher and higher above the plains, which gradually unfolded map-like below. It was a thrilling ride and a first unforgettable experience of mountain storming. The hilltops, hitherto so remote, came down to meet us, wreathed in clinging mists, which then began to hang clammily about our route. The sunshine was blotted out and a penetrating chilliness enveloped us. The mountains, so glorious from afar, lost their charm when we realised that we had virtually left our sunny Italy behind. Higher and higher we climbed, along the side of a bottomless valley billowing with cloud. Patches of snow began to appear on the hillsides and a freezing wind to whistle into the cars.

Arriving at a point where the road turned sharply, we were deposited at our mountain billets, huts buried deeply in snow. The rocky sides of the mountain showed indistinctly through the mists; a few pines, mantled in white, stood as strange sentinels to our new world. A more desolate spot would have been difficult to imagine, and we were certainly in no mood to essay such a feat. Our hut, divided horizontally to double the sleeping accommodation, was far from weatherproof, but we were packed closely enough to provide one another with sufficient warmth. In the afternoon the snow fell again and we agreed with the common Italian expression *e niente buona.*

The next morning found us for the first time marching along a mountain road amidst pines and large boulders on an icebound surface that curled up and down like a switchback. A sorry picture of amateur mountaineers we must have looked, slithering and sliding with our heavy loads on the treacherous road surface. But this was a deserted land and there were no extraneous eyes to observe our discomfiture. Later of course we would become expert, but it must be admitted that the conditions on that first morning were exceptional and that such difficulties were not to be frequently repeated. We were having an unlucky start. As a matter of fact our portage problem was shortly solved when we discovered at the roadside an abandoned sledge, on which we were able to pile our gun and ammunition. We reached the reserve position at 2.00 pm, when forty of the platoon were assigned to a small hut with half its floor missing. This had to be replaced before we could make ourselves comfortable. It was extremely cold and we felt the change from our sunny interlude at Quinto very much. The dark forbidding pines, standing like sentinels on every pocket of soil amidst the stark boulders, seemed to augur no good for the future. Yet hereabouts there were no signs of enemy activity. An Italian soldier, who passed the hut and whose French Doniger was able to translate, informed us that it was indeed a quiet sector — the enemy being far away beyond the wide stretch of No Man's Land — and that hitherto both sides had done their best to avoid one another. He said that the Italians had held these mountain positions for some time and had not been much affected by the Caporetto disaster, though of course they had been very apprehensive when they heard of the army's retreat across the plains behind them. The advent of help from the Western Allies had done much to keep up their spirits.

It was not until the late afternoon that our transport caught up with us and it was possible for tea to be served to revive our drooping spirits. From a well-constructed machine gun post in the reserve line I was able to see a little more of our position, though direction was very confusing among the hills. The post commanded a valley somewhere along which our front line was situated. All was quiet and deserted; it seemed absurd to suggest that the rugged picturesque Alpine land ahead was really a battle zone. Away in the distance there were the clustered houses of an Italian village, said to be in the hands of the enemy, while beyond that the scene culminated in a towering range of summits, which we knew must be well behind the Austrian lines. Rumour had it that we were merely holding this sector for a few days, pending the arrival of another division to take over from us.

For the two following days we stayed in the reserve position, freezing most of the time and becoming more and more depressed. It was an unfortunate introduction to a new front, which was later to prove not quite so unattractive as it did at the outset. After all, a change of this sort would have been difficult enough without the drawback of a particularly severe spell of weather.

At night, despite the smallness of our hut, we managed to introduce a brazier and this, together with the concentrated respiration of forty men, kept the temperature well above the hard frost in which we were enveloped. The days passed quietly, and somewhat boringly, with inspections and limited drills. Pack mules appeared to transport our rations. An advance party of officers and NCOs reported an absolutely lifeless frontline zone. The introduction of patrols was being mooted. There was a good deal of ammunition of strange design lying about; on the second day a ranker in the Durhams had been seriously wounded by an Italian grenade and sent back to the plains.

On the evening of 29 March, as we sat about our brazier, our spirits seemed to be touching the lowest depths. Only the fire was bright and we were grateful that at least the supply of fuel around us was inexhaustible. Only the crackling wood gave forth a comforting sound. Around us the tall ministering pines swayed and moaned woefully, whenever a strong gust of wind caught them. No mail had been received for some days. Evil rumours were in the air. They seemed to come out of nowhere and although incredible on first hearing, they gained authority as they spread from mouth to mouth, as unwelcome news is wont to do. It was said that the Germans had attacked in France and had broken through, and that our line had even swung back as far as the old Somme battlefield. This indefinite but awful tale was embroidered with even less credible details. It was all so vague and ill-formed, yet the main import was too obvious to be ignored. Frankly I did not believe it, and I tried to match the current rumours with previous impossible tall stories that had soon proved false. I belonged to the small optimistic group on this occasion. But what dismayed me more than anything was the credulity of most of my companions. They swallowed the tales of woe without mitigation and quoted as unimpeachable truth a prophesy attributed to the Kaiser that, though it had taken many ships to bring the British to France, only one would be needed to take them home. Some spoke of defeat as though it was now inevitable. To me such an idea was not merely incredible, it was impossible. I had always felt it in my bones that we could not lose, since to Britain defeat would have meant extinction, and that was why we just had to go on and on. But this evening the mountains were having their effect. Against my companions' unwarranted pessimism I could only set a dull anger towards those who had let this latest thing happen, a sure indication that my own certitude was now far from certain.

HISTORICAL NOTE: THE GERMAN SPRING OFFENSIVE IN THE WEST, 1918

With the great build-up of German forces in the West which followed the armistice with Russia, the German Commander-in-Chief, General Ludendorff, planned a grand offensive with the aim of destroying the Anglo-French armies before the Americans could arrive in force. For his first massive assault, which was to embody new features drawn from the experience of all the previous fighting, he chose the Somme sector, from the Scarpe in the north to the Oise in the south, falling on the right wing of the British line, part of which had only recently been taken over from the French and was not therefore completely integrated. It was hoped to drive a wedge between the two armies, which were still under separate commands. Against a total of 26 divisions in General Byng's Third Army and General Gough's Fifth Army in the sectors attacked, Ludendorff was able to assemble 71 divisions, as well as a truly massive artillery train.

On the morning of 21 March, after a brief but shattering bombardment of five hours duration and aided by a heavy ground mist, the German attack was launched with terrific elan. By the end of the first day a major British disaster seemed in sight. In particular Gough, on the right flank had to draw back hastily, and he was short of reserves. His troops were pressed back to the Somme, which the Germans crossed on 24 March. The following day Bapaume was captured from the Third Army and gaps began to open in the centre as well as in the right flank. By 26 March all the old hard-won battlefields of the Somme in 1916 had been occupied, and such places as

Albert and Bray, which had previously stood beyond the Germans' reach, had been captured.

Separation of the British and French commands had led to defective liaison. Now the two governments were impelled to appoint the French General Foch as generalissimo, with the task of co-ordinating the action of the Allied armies on the Western Front. The Germans had thus lost an immense advantage, as events were soon to show.

The Second Battle of the Somme continued, but British and French reserves were now moving into the gaps and Allied resistance was stiffening. At this juncture, on 28 March, Ludendorff launched a further offensive to the north of the Somme between the Scarfe and Vimy Ridge, with the object of driving through to the Channel at Boulogne. It happened that the nine German divisions forming the spearhead of this massive assault came up against four of the best remaining British divisions, representing all the ingredients of our army — regulars, territorials and New Army. The German attack was skilful and launched with their usual vigour; the prize before their eyes was final victory in the north, but they were met with such resolution and elasticity that by nightfall of the first day Ludendorff stopped the operation out of hand, and his chance of a great victory vanished.

Elsewhere the tide had turned. The great offensive closed on 5 April. The Germans tired out, had outrun their artillery and most of their transport. Not only had their losses been enormous but Allied reinforcements, thrown against unconsolidated positions, were exacting more and more casualties. The enemy had inflicted some 240,000 losses on the Allies at a cost at least as great to himself.

At this time the Italian front was a relative backwater. The British divisions, now transferred to the Asiago Plateau up in the Alps, were destined for an offensive on the new front, partly to strengthen a somewhat weak Allied position and partly to forestall an enemy offensive in the spring. But the great offensive in France, throwing new pressures upon Allied reserves, was to lead to this plan being abandoned.

6: ON THE ASIAGO PLATEAU

We had in fact arrived on the boundaries of the Asiago Plateau, key-point in the mountain line, over which some of the severest fighting of the war between the Italians and the Austrians had taken place. In the Sette Communi, the area of the Seven Communes, once a German ethnological pocket buried within the Italian-speaking valleys, the Austrian line ran within ten miles of the plains, which at the spot before Asiago, not far from our entry point, could have been commanded by a mere enemy advance of three miles.

To reach the British positions, as we have already seen, steep zigzagging roads climbed up from the plains over a general slope of 1 in 10. On the fringe, where the reserve positions were sited, there was a line of steep summits, ranging up to between 4,500 and 5,000 feet — very high country compared with anything the majority of us had known at home. Only members from Cumberland, Wales or the Highlands would have experienced anything with which to compare this precipitous territory, and in any case the hurried rise from the sun-bathed levels of Lombardy made the experience quite unique to most of us, adding difficulties of adjustment by its very suddenness. From this outer fringe the ground sloped down three miles in a series of rugged pine-clad folds to the edge of the plateau. The latter is a shallow basin, measuring seven miles from east to west and three miles from north to south at a general level of 3,300 feet above sea level. On our side there were no large open spaces except those about the village of Cesuna and a clearing on the slopes of Monte Kaberlaba.

The British front line ran along the foot of these wooded slopes where they came down to the edge of the plateau. The enemy line crossed the plateau from west to east at a distance of at least half a mile and in some places as much as a mile from the British trenches. The Italians had engineered the trench system in a big way, by blasting the rocks and setting up substantial defence posts. The weakness of the Allied position rested in the narrowness of the ledge between the front line and the mountain rim behind us. There was no room for manoeuvre. The nature of the ground made it difficult to position and sight the field guns, clearings in the pines often having to be made around the gun positions with the risk of exposing them to the enemy. There were certainly excellent positions for the heavies, many of which were still manned by the Italians, but, in the case of withdrawal, further support from these would have been rendered impossible by the immediate drop to the plains. An important characteristic of the Asiago sector, one that certainly determined its particular vulnerability and made it the key-point in the mountain line, was its uniqueness in affording territory over which the normal, and at that time most effective, methods of attack could be employed. Without straining the parallel too much — for some of the differences were fundamental — Asiago could be regarded as the Ypres of the Italian line.

The Asiago sector was served by three well-engineered roads leading up from the plains, numerous hairpin bends causing considerable trouble; especially at the outset, when they were still inexperienced, to our motor drivers, who were not used to this type of route. Communications across the mountain rim were difficult; runners and visual signalling had to be widely used. Field telegraph and telephone wires and cables could not be buried in the ground; in some parts the lower branches of the pines were simply festooned with hanging wires. There were also *teleferiche* cable railways up from the plains, on the chair-lift principle, but these were found in practice suitable only for the transport of ammunition.

This was the strange land we had now entered.[5]

Our occupancy of these first positions was indeed very temporary, for on 30 April units of the 7th Division came up to take over the left sub-sector, leaving the 23rd with only the right sub-sector. The two divisions now in the line were being supported by the 48th Division in the reserve area around Trissino at the foot of the mountains.

Thus we found ourselves on the road again. Our route skirted the flank of a steep slope clothed with pine trees. Gaps on our left were masked with camouflage, through which we obtained extensive views across a wide valley to the distant mountain range, all of which we knew was in enemy hands. With the sun shining brilliantly beyond the trees there was a strange austere beauty about our surroundings, which refuted any suggestion that this was a battlefield. Eventually the road ran into a valley and later at a road junction, called Pria dell'Acqua, we turned at right-angles away from the line. Henceforward the route went up and down like a switchback between hills whose pine-covered slopes accommodated the

---

[5] The *Official History* summarises the actual operation by the 23rd Division in the following paragraph: 'The move forward towards the line began on 26th March; on the 27th the 68th Brigade took over the sub-sector of the line from the Italian 12th Division; on the 28th the 70th Brigade took over the right sub-sector from the Italian 11th Division, and the 69th Brigade moved into the Granezza area (4 miles south of Asiago) as divisional reserve. At 12 noon on 29th March the GOC 23rd Division took over from the Italian XXVI Corps, with headquarters at Lonedo (9 miles south of Asiago).'

huts and shacks of Italian troops, doing duty there as gunners and supply groups. From gun pits dug in behind breastworks the muzzles of their heavies protruded. At one spot not far from Pria dell'Acqua a complete saw-mill had been set up. It was hard at work continuously adding sawn timbers to the stacks already standing at the roadside. The air was heavy with the resinous smell of cut wood.

At length we reached a large clearing, where the hills parted to create a miniature plain, on which a camp of crude hutments, now somewhat dilapidated in appearance, had been established. This was Granezza, our new temporary home, looking dreary enough on our arrival, amidst an expanse of snow.

We were welcomed by a real bread ration, our first for some days, but otherwise there was little to enthuse over. At that time of year Granezza was a cheerless place. The day after our arrival being Easter Sunday, we formed up in the snow for church parade and gradually froze. I'm afraid there was as much cursing as praying, but the Padre did his best. That same evening, I discovered the military theatre, a neat all-wood building constructed by the Italian army, where the band of the West Yorkshire Regiment provided a concert of popular music, which was well appreciated by an audience of all ranks.

On the following day, appropriately the first of April, there was a different sort of diversion. During a previous night a British patrol had stumbled upon an enemy advance post comfortably occupying a house in No Man's Land. Oblivious of the rules of the game in this sector, our troops had straight away taken all the Austrians prisoner and brought them back to our lines. To signalise their appreciation of this 'heroic' exploit our Allies had bestowed medals on the officer and NCOs of the patrol, and it was to be our good fortune to witness the ceremony. We were marched to a clearing hard by the junction where the road led off towards Pria dell'Acqua, drawn up in square formation amidst the boulders and there left standing, not even knowing at the time what was in the air. Standing in the snow, we waited, getting colder and colder; then a drizzling rain began to fall. We were quickly soaked to the skin and so numbed that it was difficult to hold our rifles. At long last a car drew up, from which an Italian general alighted, a short dapper little man in spick and span blue uniform decorated with many stars and bright ribbons. We saluted, grinding our teeth as our numbed fingers slipped down the rifle stocks. The victims were drawn up, duly decorated and kissed, while we presented arms once again. It was a theatrical performance that would have been really funny in more propitious circumstances. When we got back to our huts the sea of snow was already changing into a filthy greyish slush.

Our particular job at this station was to mount anti-aircraft guard and to while away the monotonous hours as best we could. One evening, to a noisily appreciative audience, our Divisional Concert Party, The Dumps, gave a most effective revue, *Niente* (Italian for 'Nothing'). It was a rollicking show, which did credit to both the performers and the producer. The army authorities were clearly doing their best to keep up the morale of the troops in very depressing circumstances. Unfortunately, the news from France was bad. The enemy, we heard, were still forging ahead. Our only consolation was that we were not personally involved in the cataclysm — yet. Depressing news about the war, temperatures much lower than we had been used to, the infernal desolation of the black pine forests: we had at that time little cause to be cheerful. To while away the time enthusiasts resorted to the game of pontoon, which, after pay-day, was the most effective way of causing hut timbers to re-echo and the money to change hands. As the evening wore on wrangling among the players increased and the rest of us were kept awake far into the night by the altercations: all strictly against rules after 'lights out', of course.

Our days were spent in helping the other army services, one of the immemorial functions of the infantry. One day we went up the mountainside to clean up the Italian defence lines and make the trenches shipshape in case of emergency. The work was directed by benevolent members of the Royal Engineers one of whom, a sergeant, told us of an interesting furlough visit he had recently made to Rome. How I envied him this experience, which was something well beyond the financial resources of a mere infantryman. The following day took us all the way to Pria dell'Acqua to unload six-inch shells for a new British heavy battery, which was being dug in in the vicinity. These shells, weighing the best part of a hundredweight, were a tremendous burden for us to move, even over short distances, and the majority of us were soon knocked up. On another occasion we went along to a near-by dump to unload the supply waggons of a column that never arrived. We grumbled when the work was tiring; we grumbled when it was easy but monotonous; we grumbled even more when led out like this on a fool's errand. We never knew where we were. That of course was the army all over.

One morning we were told to put on drill order with haversack for a visit to divisional baths at the foot of the mountains. I was surprised to discover how near we were at Granezza to the very edge of the plateau. We had barely left the clearing, when we passed through the low hill barrier by which the valley was surrounded, and found ourselves looking down steeply to the plains, which seemed to spread about us as the road wound downwards. It was unexpected and exciting.

At first we walked down steep paths through wild rugged country, strewn with boulders and crossed by rushing torrents. Then a change came and warmer vegetation began to clothe the hillsides. Hereabouts little white-walled hamlets clung to the steep banks as though preparing at the least provocation to leap down into the valley below. The main road, in every way a massive engineering feat, moved downwards in slow measured gradients. We left the clouds behind, clambering down short-cut paths connecting the zigzags and entered at last a land of flowers, rich verdure and running waters. The wonder of a lovely world soon took hold of us.

We bivouacked in Italian tents in a meadow on the bank of a stream, and enjoyed the sylvan tranquillity of the place in brilliant sunshine. We seemed to be at least a hundred miles away from the battle line along the top of that steep green wall reaching far above us. We had our refreshing bath and made a visit to the over-flowing divisional canteen set up in the neighbouring village of Fara. The contrast between our two worlds was hardly credible.

We took our time in climbing back, halting in a small mountain village on the following day, some in houses, others in bivouacs on the hillside. I was among the latter. That night there was much drinking and pandemonium in the camp, the revellers constantly falling over guy ropes and banging the sides of the tents to discover the whereabouts of their pals. Then a storm, which had been gathering for some time, as they do in mountainous country, broke in full force upon us. In the darkness of the night the rain came swishing down, while the wind roared with gale force. Many of the bivouacs were washed or blown away; the rains soaked into most of the others. We were fortunate in being able to keep ours erect until the morning. The rest of our journey upwards was far from comfortable. The rain continued, and the going amidst the boulders was often treacherous. Though the storm had abated by the time we reached Granezza, the huts and trees there were wreathed in clammy mist, and in our bedraggled state we felt that a pleasant interlude had been sadly spoiled by the elements, of whose powers we had been given a most spectacular demonstration. Hot tea and rum were served to stave off more serious consequences.

There was a heavy fall of snow during that night and on the following day — 11 April — we went into the line again. Our division was taking over the right sector, which we reached by branching rightwards from Pria dell'Acqua. We passed through the supply lines in the valley amidst the pines, heavy batteries manned by Italians and our own various service corps getting acclimatised to the very new conditions. All stores had to be brought up the tracks, threading under the trees, either by pack mule or human porterage. The slushy snow, dreary dripping trees and the tiring meandering paths quickly brought it home to us that conditions in our new battleground were not going to be exactly a picnic. The Durham Light Infantry had casualties on the way. Shells bursting amidst the trees brought back all the old sensations of going into the trenches in France, and we felt particularly exposed on the hillsides, where there was no trench cover.

The company took over the reserve positions, situated on a hillside track running parallel to the summit a short distance above, with the valley well below us. At first we were assigned to a shelter which looked like a disused gun pit. Through a gaping opening on the north side we could look over the plateau, but the scene was blotted out by waves of driving rain, which saturated the shelter and also fell in melancholy splashes from the trees. The enemy must have been aware that

119

something was afoot for he began a steady bombardment. The shells screamed over, to burst among the trees on the opposite slope of the valley behind us. We were not sorry therefore to be moved to a somewhat less exposed position a little way up the track to the right, where it passed under the shelter of the summit. Our new shelter was a large log hut, not by any means weather-proof and situated on the wrong side of the track. The opposite, and safer, edge was fringed with dug-outs in the hillside, occupied by other troops.

Our short spell in this position was neither comfortable nor happy. During that night the Austrian artillery was mildly active, shells dropping continuously in the trees behind us. The replying bombardment from our guns was even more unsettling, for the shells seemed to be screaming up towards us, causing the branches above to crackle in sympathy before they swooped away over the ridge just above on their way to the enemy positions.

The day dawned dark and drear; our surroundings for the most part dripped with moisture. We spent the time on fatigues, tidying up and carrying, but, with plenty of time for talking and listening to rumour, we had every cause for depression. Rumour was even more disheartening than usual. Our rations had been cut because of the disaster in France. Belated reports in papers from home, which had been delayed in transit, and the tales of men who were constantly trickling back from hospital and elsewhere, all contributed to the building of a frightening picture. We also began to realise that things had been happening in France, from which we had been isolated even while we were still there.

In the previous year there had been trouble at the base at Etaples, even rioting; the worm turning at last! Members of the women's corps, the WAACS and other units, had been arriving in force. In the early days their sanitary arrangements had been very primitive. The wash-houses were exposed, as so often our own were. In our case it did not matter, but now in the case of the female the publicity was different — men were not slow in availing themselves of the opportunity offered. Apart from this natural inclination of the male to improve the shining hour, most of us were shocked by all this. After all we had not yet 'progressed', if that is the proper word, very far from Victorian ideas of propriety. The general opinion at the time was that the sending of women to share these conditions was quite unnecessary, so long as there were males at the base fit enough for the auxiliary tasks, and there was also the feeling that there were still plenty of male slackers to be combed out at home. Already the tale was going round that the authorities had other notions in sending over women to take their part. It was felt that a little more female company would help to keep up morale. We were certainly not impressed by this line of reasoning for we could see no reason why the morale of the base wallahs should require this special consideration. However, we did realise that in the minds of the people at home there was no distinction between the base and the line troops. As an example of the situation that had developed, one informant told us that when air raid warnings came during the night, and this, he said, happened rather more frequently than appeared to be strictly necessary, it was the practice to allow the troops to break camp and bivouac in the fields around. On these occasions he had seen Tommies and WAACS pairing under the same blankets. The authorities turned a blind eye upon these goings on, or appeared to do so, for in the darkness things could happen without anyone becoming too much concerned. We all took a very poor view of these reports, perhaps largely because we were dogs in the manger too far away to share in the frolics. I do not know how far it was official policy to encourage fraternisation among the lower orders in this way, with the object of meeting natural needs, keeping up morale and winning the war, but I think there must have been something in it during both the major wars, contributory factors in the changes in moral attitudes and sex relations which have undoubtedly been taking place during the present century. Other stories centred on goings on at a rest camp in Marseilles and on an army hospital there for venereal diseases, in which there was no dearth of cases. Mixed with definite authentic news of retreats on the Western Front, these other tales helped to build up a very depressing picture, particularly at a time when we found enough personal discomfort in our immediate surroundings.

But the picture painted by hearsay and personal accounts was not all black. Heartening tales of the increasing inflow of American troops into France were also gaining currency. One of our NCOs, who had been attached to an American group for a few days before returning to us, told how one Northumberland Fusilier battalion had been relieved by our new allies. They were, he said, of fine physique (contrasting particularly with our dwindling standards of physical fitness), well-equipped and filled with a superb self-confidence and eagerness to get at the Germans. We had clearly been dawdling in winning the war! But they were woefully ignorant as to what they were up against, and had a lot to learn. After only a few days in the trenches they lost a good deal of their cocksureness and began to realise that the war below ground was something more than picnics and dinner parties. Our informant was very humorous over their initial mistakes and personal reactions, and there was much laughter round the brazier when he recounted some of their initial misconceptions and errors.

Here at any rate was something to offset the gloom of the main picture and, if little was said in favour of our new allies — and I think in the main we felt that there was some criticism in their arrival at a stage when our own leaders should already have been able to ensure victory — yet the mere fact of their arriving and of the promise of vast armies to follow must have gone a long way to wipe out the depressing potentialities of immediate events.

At this time a few Italian sleeping bags were issued to the ranks. I was among the fortunate recipients, who found them wonderfully cosy at night. As new-fangled things these bags were not very popular, and I do not remember that very much use was made of them subsequently. They certainly had the grave disadvantage of slowing down one's reactions to an emergency stand-to!

The trees continued to drip, occasional shells to moan over, and general depression to reign over us. Our platoon commander had already left us for a special job while we were still on the plains and we had been sorry to lose him; for despite his shy, unmilitary demeanour he had during his brief attachment impressed us as a good sort. In his place we now received, while in this log hut, a youthful office worker hailing from Lancashire. He was a nice boy in every way, with school-girl complexion and questioning eyes. He had come straight from England, without any war experience, to take charge of as hard-bitten and experienced a crowd of old sweats as one could imagine. I was both sorry for him and utterly disgusted with a system that could work so absurdly. He was a bank clerk and belonged to the respectable class, a status no higher than my own as a civil servant. His only qualification to take charge of men in battle appears to have emanated in the mind of a doting mother, who felt that it was only right and proper for her son to be an officer. A little influence and wire-pulling had done the rest. Yet those poor misled mothers needed so much our pity, for their sacrifices in that generation were beyond all computation. Fortunately they were filled with sentiments of patriotism and ideas of glory, and knew little of what was really going on behind the active service curtain. Our new leader had little to overcome his manifest disadvantages, no authority in manner and a girlish voice. His almost superhuman efforts to sound manly were so ludicrous as to bring titters from the men, who normally did their utmost to play the game as laid down by their betters. We all knew that we were victims of a system, which somehow had emerged before our time, and in the main there was no general impulse to make matters worse for any of its victims. We wanted more than anything else to get the current job done; at the time the means mattered little. But it was still difficult to accept the reasonableness of sending such raw leaders as this to take charge of us. I do not even remember this particular victim's name, but as he was to figure in an early casualty list this is hardly surprising.

One of our duties in the reserve line was to man an SOS post in the support trench which ran beyond the ridge above us. It was an excellent position with a fine outlook over the pines, although during our first spell all that was obscured by the driving rain. Later we were able to discern the ruined town of Asiago away out on the plateau and a number of smaller hamlets or groups of buildings here and there. Our artillery was bombarding the town, which even at that distance appeared already to have been almost completely devastated. The panoramic layout presented our gunners with excellent targets; our own positions must have been much less conspicuous to the enemy, with the thick curtain of trees around us. Very naturally the Austrians were no longer leaving all offensiveness to us, although it is doubtful whether this renewed activity on a front that had recently been allowed to be quiescent was very welcome to them. Enemy shells were falling in the valley when we got back to our hut shelter, and we felt even less secure than ever. In a gun pit down the hill just below us five Italian gunners were killed and a number wounded. The Durhams sent down a seriously wounded case from the front line. We were realising that we had come back into the war with a vengeance.

On the following day (15 April) we sent back our first casualties. The desultory bombardment continued to keep us tensed up. We would have preferred to be in the actual line over the hill. The enemy shells screamed over the brow with a disconcerting rush, seeming to brush through the tree-tops above us. When they burst down in the valley or on the opposite hillside there followed a wrenching and shattering of branches and a rain of tree debris around us. There was one particularly tense moment during the afternoon when a shell actually burst against one of the trees forming the corner posts of our rag-time shelter, bringing it down with a crash on the timbered roof. Although many of us were inside at the time no one was hurt, but we were shaken up.

The danger did not come only from the enemy. The Italian gunners, replying from below, occasionally had premature bursts; whether due to the mounting shell hitting a tree before clearing the hill or to faulty fusing on their part is not possible to say, but one or two shells burst much too close to the hut for comfort. One discharge did actually take place just in front of the dugout below us, before it had got clear, making a horrible mess of two of the gun's crew. I used to feel that death or mutilation by accident in this way was even more frightening than when the enemy was responsible. It seemed outside the rules.

We had the impression that the powers-that-be were expecting something. That evening at 7 pm the company carried out a practice stand-to in the support trench to see how long it would take. Strange rumours were going round, even stranger than usual. It was said that men were to be taken from each battalion as reinforcements for France. At this rate we felt the army in Italy would gradually melt away. With all the tragic uncertainty on the French front, and the sacrifice of territory there, which had been so dearly bought with the fives of our friends and companions, we felt doubly cut off in Italy from the rest of our world. Home hardly existed for us outside our dreams. There was an insuperable barrier between. The war was lapping at us like the waves of a sea in which we should inevitably be engulfed. Surrounded by the mournful swaying trees against a background of rain-laden skies and nagged at constantly by the splitting and chattering artillery, I felt as if I were in some horrible dream, waiting...

On the following day news came that our canteen down in the valley had received supplies. No civilised amenity was missed so much as the shop-round-the-corner, and the dangers of the valley had no effect upon this shopping occasion. The small supplies of chocolate, biscuits and tinned fruits were soon being heavily requisitioned.

During the night a number of bursts in the proximity of our shelter forced us to leave our uncomfortable beds and to seek cover in an already over-crowded dug-out just opposite. We were not sorry, therefore, when the DLIs replaced us during the next afternoon and we took over their positions in the front line.

This change was very much for the better. The pine-clothed slopes rendered communication trenches both impracticable and unnecessary on this part of the front. Carrying out a relief therefore at any time of the day presented none of the normal problems. We now occupied a trench at the foot of the slope, well-blasted out of the solid rock and equipped with a respectable dug-out. We were still among the trees, but to our right the trench passed out across a bare gulley to disappear again amidst trees on the far side. Generally the line seemed to zigzag in and out of the edge of the forests which fringed the southern borders of the Asiago Plateau. Our field of observation straight ahead was good, though we could see little either to left or right. Shattered houses stood out in the middle distance, in front of a more considerable place, beyond which the opposite slopes climbed up to the dark forests that clothed the lower flanks of the impressive mountain range, whose high jagged peaks were capped with glistening snow. We could see the lines made by the roads as they ran up into the valleys, and we knew that over there the enemy faced us in a position not very dissimilar from ours, if rather less insecure, and was experiencing similar difficulties.

Strategically, of course, the two positions were very different. If we pushed the Austrian he had hundreds of miles of difficult mountain country to fall back upon; if he pushed us we should quickly flow over the edge of the range beyond Granezza, and drop a sheer three thousand feet on to the plains below.

We spent our days on gas guard in the trench and our nights with the Lewis gun out on advance post, in front of the rocks at the end of the gully, where we had a much wider field of fire. This was a fatiguing routine, particularly with the low rations which we were at that time receiving. I have no doubt that the main cause for this was the difficulty of organising effective supply lines up into the mountains. The points of entry were limited. Our stretcher bearers were ordered to rub everyone's feet with oil as a precaution against frost bite. Sock putties, which had been issued for use in the trenches but found useless, were collected. During this period the troops were getting frantic over the shortage of tobacco; tea leaves were again being rolled into cigarettes and smoked with apparent enjoyment. It was not pleasant to witness the tortures of those who were in the grip of this craving, but I felt that I was doubly fortunate in being a non-smoker, even if I did miss some unsampled pleasure when supplies were more abundant.

On our second night in the front positions, which was a wet one, a company patrol made contact with the enemy and there was a lively exchange of rifle and trench mortar fire, but there were no casualties on this occasion. A couple of nights later one of our patrols did suffer a casualty, apparently inflicted by one of our own men. This was hardly surprising; out in the darkness amidst the confining shadows of the boulders everything was very confusing, particularly in the absence of the normal, sometimes, gruesome landmarks of a Western Front battlefield. The possibility of a first-class scrap springing up among friendly groups was ever present to heighten nervous tensions.

It was during this spell in the line that I struck up a particularly close friendship with old Tom Ireland, the company's veteran who, nearing middle age, was certainly old enough to be my father. I remember him from the earliest days in Canada Street, in front of Ypres, where members of his recently arrived draft from home had joined us in an old German pillbox. On this present occasion I particularly remember one of our few fine days when the sun shone down on our trench, beautifying even the tall dark trees and filling the keen mountain air with a promise of spring. We stood on the fire-step of our deep trench, surrounded by those wonderful hills, and for a few unapprehensive moments it was good to be alive again. Tom, his generous soul expanding in the sunshine, spoke of his younger days and amorous adventures in distant Bradford. How one evening he and a friend picked up a couple of girls, only for him to be assigned the plain one. His pal's beauty gave him the pox. He spoke in happiness of his good wife, whose ministering kindness had so often been manifested in her lovingly packed parcels, which he so generously shared. All over Britain at that time motherly women, lonely women, hiding an endless heartache, were for ever packing with loving fingers those carefully thought-out parcels to the front. We each looked forward to our own especial package and none was more welcomed than the budget of good things that came regularly from that poor Bradford home, put together at who knows what sacrifice in those poverty-stricken times. During these trench conversations the years between us were as nothing and our friendship ripened. On one such afternoon I remember that our talk had left me in a state of happy reverie upon a future that might one day become reality, when a trickle of shells from the enemy side brought me instantly to earth. The strong solidity of our trench was reassuring enough, though indeed the hard chips of rock thrown up by the explosions promised to assist the shrapnel in its deadly work. As usual, the enemy strafe did not last long.

The rain returned and this turned to snow, making our advance post vigil very uncomfortable. We were not sorry, therefore, when we arrived back at our dug-out on the morning of 22 April, to be welcomed with the news that the 48th Division were taking over the sector. Later in the day we went back to Granezza, now much more lively than previously. Already there was a fully equipped YMCA in operation.

Our stay at Granezza was brief, for the next day, the feast of St George, on which we exercised the regimental privilege of wearing red and white rosettes in our caps, found us on our way to the plains. It was a beautiful morning with clearer skies than we had seen since our arrival in the mountains. All around us, forming a vast amphitheatre, were the hills and mountains of the Alpine fringe, a glorious scene into which we descended with jolting steps but the lightest of hearts, towards the plains stretched below us like an immense carpet, towns and villages, rivers and streams, fields and roads showing up map-like in the brilliant sunshine in a patchwork of a dozen shades of green. We descended until, amidst the rolling foothills, we again reached Fara, now with its two large army canteens, stocked with English food of all kinds.

The next day found us in a bivouac in a field about eleven kilometres further back, where we encountered a tremendous thunderstorm, which collected rapidly and literally swept down upon us from the mountains. This natural artillery display was awe-inspiring and terrible, but it receded as quickly as it had approached and all was calm again. Our next halt was in the village of Tezze, over thirty kilometres away — a gruelling march in the brilliant sunshine, as hot as an English mid-summer day. I had been feeling off colour, owing no doubt to the sudden change from mountain to plain, cool to heat, semi-starvation to comparative luxury.

Tezze itself has left no picture in my mind, although we stayed there for two or three days. This was no doubt partly due to my still feeling unwell, partly to the fact that there was nothing disagreeable about the place to impress it on my memory. I do remember a trip out on the second day, which took us to an asylum on the road into Montecchio Maggiore, where army baths had been installed, without interfering too much with its normal inmates. Some of them, occupied in the kitchen garden at the rear, appeared to pay little heed to the strange humans in foreign uniforms, speaking an incomprehensible tongue. No doubt we fitted into their scheme of things quite logically! But as we left after our refreshing bathe one of the inmates at least showed that he had detected something stranger than usual, and registered well-warranted disapproval by aiming a rotten apple at the marching column from an upper window. Or was this the authentic soldier's farewell?

The village of Montecchio Maggiore is impressively situated at the foot of a range of hills, two of whose nearer summits are capped by the ruins of castles attributed to the Scaligeri, a noble family of mediaeval Verona, and are said to be the source of the legend of Romeo and Juliet. These imposing battlements can be discerned from the railway by travellers going to Venice via Verona, as seen they were by us on a number of occasions during our military wanderings about the foothills.

On the last day of April, after a tiring march of two days — tiring because of the sweltering sun rather than the actual distances covered — we found billets in a small village perched amidst a range of pleasant hills, which rose up from the plains about twenty miles south-east of Vicenza. From a small inadequate map purchased locally, I gathered that these were the Euganei Hills. We were comfortably billeted in really delightful surroundings. The weather in the plains was getting so hot that we were now parading in shirt-sleeves. For some days my internal unrest had continued and I had not been very happy. Doniger suggested that I was suffering from a surfeit of bully beef stew. I accepted his advice of switching over to a diet of green vegetables, a line of conduct that was made possible then, as at no other time during my war experience, by the abundance of fruit and greenstuffs to be purchased locally. I have a note that lettuce and spring onions could be bought in the village. Improvement in my digestion followed almost immediately and it is clear that our heavy-handed army organisation was proving quite incapable of coping with such changes in circumstance as we were then experiencing. Another note in my diary reported a swallow-tail butterfly on the wing, which I had seen when skirmishing over the hills, a sure sign that I was again taking a hundred per cent interest in what was going on around me.

I had grown to admire Doniger for many reasons. A Jew, kindly, studious and generous, much less warlike in spirit than I, and with a brilliant sense of economy, he stood out among my companions. The latter trait often led to his being imposed upon. Borrowing and lending were always going on in the ranks, to tide over to pay day, especially among the gamblers, who spent much of their spare time in billets playing brag and pontoon. Doniger never refused to lend a few *lire*, but unfortunately some of his less scrupulous borrowers, instead of repaying him on pay day, were in the habit of taunting him with offensive statements, which was both unreasonable and unjust. I should have flown into a temper at once, but Doniger received every set-back calmly and made little fuss about his bad debts. One day about that time I remember getting myself into hot water by reproving some of these dishonest borrowers. I just couldn't contain myself any longer. But little came of my somewhat disingenuous attempt at knight errantry. Morally my friend's conduct was splendid.

On Sunday 12 May, by way of innovation — for we were still told little about what was happening in the military world around us — an officer lectured us on the characteristics of the Austrian machine gun. He was sufficiently lucid and well-informed to make the subject interesting and, needless to say, this slight departure from the normal attitude of the authorities was appreciated. During the evening I sat with my back against a large stone in the dreary cul-de-sac by the billet. The sun continued to shine, atoning for the shabbiness of the human habitations around us. Some of the inhabitants of the cottages, old men missed by conscription's broom, were amusing themselves throwing their knives at a sun-cracked front door. They were obviously proud of their marksmanship, as indeed they had good right to be, for is not the clasp knife, or rather the stiletto, the Italian's historic weapon? The skilful throwing was being watched with interest by a number of Tommies who had not chosen to go off on a scrounge with the majority. Eventually one of them conceived the idea of emulating the Italians with his bayonet. His first throw was successful; very soon quite half a dozen khaki-clad figures were hurling their bayonets at the door in the approved manner. This was as successful as the preceding knife-throwing had been and much more spectacular. The Italians watched with open-eyed astonishment, wondering no doubt over this unexpected accomplishment, for which members of the British army obviously received training!

It was another week before we moved back towards the line and our stay in the hills continued to be made worthwhile, despite other shortcomings, by the wonderful sunshine. Everything seemed to promise a fruitful summer and the natural beauty was a sad contrast to the human devilry in which we were involved. Not that everyone found good reason to rejoice. The countryfolk were poor enough, as was strikingly brought home to me one evening when I watched them skinning frogs for the frying pan.

One of our second lieutenants chose this moment to tighten up the censorship of letters, an activity which I never regarded with favour, though no doubt it was necessary. It was generally recognised that we should not describe our personal experiences or state where we were; now it seemed that there was to be a ban on our saying how we felt. A member of the company wrote that he was fed up and hoped that the war would soon be over. Who indeed did not feel and wish as much? The officious censor told him that this was information of interest to the enemy and likely to dishearten the people at home. The writer was 'put on the peg', but the case was dismissed. No doubt orders had been issued for the censors to take special care, in view of the general war situation, but there are right and wrong ways of complying with such instructions.

19 May found us back in the reserve huts in the mountains near the road junction of Pria dell'Acqua. Our ramshackle hut was far from weather-proof and lucky were those of us who managed to lay out their kits under a sound section of the roof. At brigade headquarters, on the opposite side of the road to us, a ceremonial guard had been posted, which was smart enough for Buckingham Palace. From mere observation one would not have guessed that we were close to the front line. It was a pity that there was no one to see it all.

The weather in the heights had certainly improved during our absence. A brilliant sun shone without being oppressive, a soft balmy breeze blew through the glades between the pines, and on all sides spring flowers poked up out of the carpet of moss and pine cones. It would have been good to be alive, had not the marshalled pine trunks created the impression of hiding something sinister and insecure.

Our rations too were improved. They now included rice and oatmeal, while the butter ration had been increased. Sometimes I managed to supplement my store by the purchase of a loaf from an Italian soldier, member of one of the supply units or gun teams camped among us. This was so filling that a small loaf was sufficient to supplement one's white bread ration for two or three days. The Italian army was obviously badly off for food; this close-grained bread and the red wine in large casks, that came up on specially constructed trucks rather like ladders on wheels, seemed to be their main diet. Like ourselves they had their own dodges to improve the position and it was by no means unusual to see a chicken-run behind their gun-pit, a domestic touch sadly out of tune there.

We spent our days on the usual drills, bayonet fighting, standing to in the reserve trenches up the hillside, and in occasional hill climbs, which were very fatiguing to us flatlanders. Our exercises were carried out among the trees, wherever a suitable clearing could be found, but the pines and firs grew close and such open spaces were few and far between. One evening the valley was overwhelmed by a terrific storm; fierce lightning flashes pierced the gloom under the driving rain and a heavy tree crashed down the hillside not far away. The trees swayed before the blast like grass and the world outside our billet assumed an appearance of terrifying grandeur. Inside we stood with faces lit up by the vivid flashes, overawed yet elated by the spectacle. The storm passed as it had arisen; deliciously cool mountain air wafted through the woods, bringing an indescribable freshness, as the stars above the gently swaying treetops sparkled out in a sky of the deepest turquoise. But nature had claimed at least one victim: an artilleryman in a neighbouring cabin had been killed by lightning.

One day — it was 22 May — I was surprised by an unexpected 'promotion', when I was raised from the position of Number Three to Number One on the platoon's Lewis gun. Westgarth, who had been Number One for so long, had recently left us with a stripe to take over a rifle section. Thus, Weatherall and Hardcastle were the next in seniority for the positions of Number One and Number Two. Always argumentative and addicted to well-meaning horseplay, they had seemed to lose cohesion when their close pal, Golightly, had been killed in the autumn. Now the transfer of Westgarth left them stranded. At this present juncture they fell foul of the company's Lewis gun sergeant, normally a very urbane Scotsman and close friend of us all, by disobeying an instruction while on parade. Saying that there was to be no more nonsense, he instructed me to take charge forthwith. There was something about the change that gave it the appearance of being cut-and-dried, although it came as a complete surprise to me. The two demoted ones took the blow quite philosophically and to deny that I felt a certain elation would be disingenuous. On the other hand, if it had not thus been sprung upon me, or I had had any choice on the spot, I am sure I should have avoided my new charge.

However, I decided after a little argument in my mind that the change did not really go against my attitude to promotion. I was still but a full-blown private; although the Number One of the Lewis gun team had certain privileges, which made the job even more attractive than that of a junior NCO. In future I should discard my rifle and carry a revolver[6] and therefore not

---

[6] At this stage of the war the Number One of the Lewis Gun team was the only ranker to carry a revolver.

have the trouble of shouldering arms and carrying out all the other arms drills on parade or on the march, and I should henceforth be exempted from many fatigues. I was now a privileged specialist. In exchange for all this, it would be my duty to see that the gun was always in good order and to handle it personally in action. With this new responsibility, the feeling of being a key-man, some subtle change began to take place within me. This is clear in retrospect, though I was hardly aware of it at the time.

On the same day heavy Austrian shells fell in the vicinity of the huts, emphasising the insecurity of the position. The slope of the ground and the clustering trees seemed to affect the missile's trajectory, so that we could never assess when it was going to burst. Often these shells seemed to be caught in flight and to burst prematurely as they were approaching. On the hillsides bursts were always erratic and the normal process of flattening oneself to the ground, that had become an automatic reaction in France, was of little avail. With this change a certain sense of security, that may often have had little foundation, was lost.

It was reported that fever had broken out in the 23rd Division and that a number of cases had been sent to hospital. This was the first definite news we had had about the flu epidemic which was ravaging Europe at the time and was sometimes referred to in the south as Alpine fever. Recently the weather had been improving. Some of our artillerymen had already been issued with drill uniforms, which we understood were to be the normal wear for us all during the summer months.

On all sides increasing military activity was apparent and rumours of a forthcoming drive were generally accepted. After all, we had had a long quiet spell since leaving Passchendaele and there seemed to be every reason to expect a thrust at the enemy sooner rather than later. At the same time there was increasing activity in the air; our planes seemed to be everywhere and were constantly making trips over enemy positions. One day leaflets, printed in what we took to be a Slavonic language, fell in the camp, obviously intended for the enemy. Then there was a lecture on map reading, followed by a demonstration at a large-scale model of the Asiago Plateau, on which the two trench lines were set out in clear relief. All these signs pointed only in one direction, although this was not very clear to us at the time. As usual we were not let into any secrets about the plans that were maturing at army headquarters.

On Sunday 26 May we returned by the mule track over the heights to relieve the Durhams in support. Viewed in the light of our experience in France, the situation on this front had something of a comic opera about it. We now occupied dugouts and bivouacs set amidst the rocky ground some way up the hillside. Mule tracks led away in all directions, while between us and the enemy a solid wall of trees blotted out all observation. Our only task was to man a combined gas guard and anti-aircraft post. Italian soldiers from the batteries and supply corps in the vicinity came round selling nougat and chocolate at very high prices; they had learned our weaknesses and were out to make as much as they could. I tried to buy bread on behalf of the section but it was too scarce and precious at this time to be traded.

The weather turned showery and the rain soon percolated through the rocky ground and penetrated our log-covered shelter. We found it impossible to keep dry. One night one of our front-line patrols fell foul of the enemy and suffered as many as eleven casualties, including the officer, with another missing. The body of the missing man was brought in on the following night.

At breakfast on 30 May we heard a whirring of many propellors and above the pines saw a magnificent fleet of at least thirty aeroplanes sailing northwards over the plateau. A lull followed, during which we were busily occupied with our frugal meal of a rasher of bacon and a dish of tea from the cookhouse, with some hard biscuits and jam, and we then prepared our equipment to move off. Far away in the distance we heard the thuds of dropping bombs. Then our machines returned, as majestically as they had sailed over, away to the sunshine of the plains. At that time this impersonal war was indeed new and there were some of us who felt more akin to our enemy in the lines opposite than to our own bombing experts.

That day we returned to the front line position, with ourselves, Number 6 Platoon, in close support. We occupied a lean-to shelter of tree trunks built against a grassy bank, comfortable but not shell-proof. This was in a beautiful clearing at the bottom of a miniature ravine. The ground was carpeted with sweet-smelling mosses and rotting pine cones, while here and there sprinklings of alpine flowers or splashes of bracken added colour to the scene. The sun shone through the over-hanging branches, speckling the ground with a bright mosaic of refracted light. Ever and anon this delightful illusion of woodland beauty was broken by the metallic bark of a field gun echoing along the timbered aisles; awakened out of my dream, I remembered that the war was still on.

The platoon sergeant, chatting with me on one of his rounds, told me about a scheme to give leave in the form of a short stay at Sermione on the shores of Lake Garda, where a special rest-house had been equipped. He wondered whether I would like an early place on the list. I was interested but wary. Such a spell in the sunshine away from the front had its obvious attractions, but deep in my heart was the longing to visit a more distant place, coupled with a fear that acceptance of a lesser bounty might prejudice the greater when it became due. In any case, when the trips to Lake Garda did materialise, difficulties soon arose. The men at the rest-house, too effusively welcomed by the ladies of the town, were soon furnishing an excessive number of patients for the army hospitals, and for safety's sake the arrangements had to be suspended.

When the month of June began, we were out on patrol between the lines. No Man's Land hereabouts was very hilly, and the night was filled with fantastic shadows, thrown out by the walls of boulders that divided the fields and tracks, or with the occasional gaunt shape of a derelict building, sticking up, white and ghostly, into the twilight. Behind us our own positions were shrouded in the darkness of the massed pines, whose tops only were silhouetted against the starry sky. In front the plateau rolled away in billows that seemed much steeper in the night than they really were. For most of the time everything was quiet — except for the exaggerated clatter of our feet against every loose stone, as we patrolled cautiously between the spurs. Every shadow-making boulder was a promising hiding place for lurking foes — though clearly the Austrians, unlike the Germans, were not habitually in lurking mood. Over towards the enemy positions, well in front of Asiago town, all was still. Yet we knew that the enemy was also on the prowl and holding strong points not far away. Towards the morning our presence was detected and we were subjected to a bombardment of rifle-grenades, which whirled over with a peculiarly hesitating swish and burst spitefully among the rocks. We withdrew at daybreak without a casualty.

At this season the woods were now awake with nature. Birds of all kinds fluttered amidst the branches or soared above the stretching pines. Often I heard the home-like cuckoo, rejoicing no doubt over his successful imposture. That very morning of the first of June I spotted an eagle on the wing, flying mightily towards the distant mountains, while on a tree outside our timbered billet an industrious woodpecker tapped away. I remembered the Salient and the Somme, and felt how ungrateful we were to grumble at our present lot.

On the evening of the same day we stood to, while 'C' Company raided an enemy strongpoint — a fortified house with a trench system coming up inconveniently close to our lines. Our men lay out in front of the position while the artillery dropped a heavy barrage about it. Three prisoners were taken without the necessity of storming and there were no casualties. The enemy's guns replied on our front line but the storm was over in a few minutes and could hardly be called serious.[7]

Within a few days the NCOs of 'C' Company who had taken part were decorated by the divisional general before us all, no doubt as a measure of general encouragement. We felt at the time that the indiscriminate distribution of medals for a purely routine performance of this sort was bound to detract from the value of awards more truly earned. Clearly this policy of generous and expeditious awards had an effect upon the ranks quite different from what the authorities intended.

---

[7] According to the *Official History* there were only two prisoners and the enemy suffered at least ten casualties. The former may well be true — I can only record what I heard at the time — but it is difficult to understand how even the authorities could be sure about the latter.

We were out on patrol again the following night, getting up so close to the enemy that we could hear the coughs and movements of his sentries not far away. We had to crawl forward with the Lewis gun to take up a position commanding a cross road, where it was necessary to lie still all through the night. Most of the time, as Number One, I was wondering how it would be if I had to open fire. Our artillery kept up a desultory bombardment. It was cold and very dark, except when an enemy light popped and illuminated the boulder-strewn ground around us. Now and again we heard the drone and clatter of distant transport behind the enemy lines. He was busy.

On 3 June we again returned to Granezza, now an even more bustling military junction. The weather had turned cold again and one afternoon in a snowstorm I watched a football match between the 7th and 48th Divisions, for a cup, which the former won. Fortunately for us this climatic setback did not continue, for at 5 pm on 8 June the Lewis gun section went up to man an anti-aircraft post on the heights overlooking the Granezza clearing to the north and the vast plains of the Po spreading away southwards. This was really a pleasant rest cure in the renewed sunshine. We had brought rations, amply supplemented by delicacies from the canteen, for the twenty-four hour picnic. The time passed uneventfully, except for a slight reconnaissance by an enemy plane, which was quickly frightened away by the white puffs of bursting artillery shells. It was too far away for us to waste our ammunition. On the evening of our return to the camp below there was a football match between our 10th Battalion and the RAMC, which ended in a draw.

HISTORICAL NOTE: THE AUSTRIAN OFFENSIVE OF JUNE 1918

In France, by the summer, the German offensive had been extended in three new stages or thrusts: to the Lys on 9 April, to the Aisne on 17 May and to the Matz on 6 June. Each new drive repeated more or less the pattern of the Second Battle of the Somme. The Aisne offensive had brought two American divisions into action for the first time at Chateau Thierry, where they helped to halt the German advance. The final onslaught on 9 June was frustrated by a Franco-American counterattack delivered two days later.

At this stage the enemy were ready to bring the Italian front into the picture again. Here the Austrian plan included four separate thrusts, designed to shift the Allies off the mountains and to pierce the Italian line along the Piave. The first thrust by two divisions was made on 13 June on the extreme left of the Italian positions at the Tonale Pass, and failed. On 15 June two other thrusts were made in the mountains on the Asiago and Monte Grappa sectors, also without lasting success, but the main drive across the Piave between the Montello and the sea, launched at the same time, proved more promising.

The Asiago attack, described from the author's viewpoint in the text, involved Italian troops on the left, the entire 48th Divisional front in the centre and part of the 23rd Divisional front on the right. As it happened this part of the Austrian offensive forestalled a limited Allied attack in the same sector, timed for 18 June, for which British batteries had been pushed forward close to the front line. The enemy barrage began at 3 am, much to our surprise, and according to the Official History

British batteries were ordered to carry out counter preparation beyond the outpost line at 3.30 am and to lay a defensive barrage at 5 am. It is clear that on the hinge between the Northumberland Fusiliers and the 48th Division, as mentioned in the text, our guns were silenced from the outset, owing apparently to a complete breakdown of communications. It is agreed that the 48th Division, which received the brunt of the attack, was taken completely by surprise and the Oxford Light Infantry (on the Northumberlands' left), the Gloucesters and the Royal Warwicks were quickly overrun. They were able to make a great stand on switch lines and to restore the line later, even to occupy more advanced positions by the end of the day. Allied requests to follow up these successes were turned down by the Italian Supreme Command because of a lack of reserves. To the right of this attack, on the other slope of Monte Kaberlaba, a more limited but powerful thrust had fallen upon the Sherwood Foresters, who found themselves enfiladed and compelled to fall back. The situation was restored by a counterattack, in which the Sherwood Foresters' CO, Lieutenant-Colonel C. E. Hudson, won the Victoria Cross.

Along the Piave line the Austrians were rather more successful, and for a time the position was precarious. A breakthrough there would have meant a general withdrawal from the mountains and probably the abandonment of the Plain of Lombardy right down to the Apennines.

The Austrians were handicapped through having dispensed with thorough artillery spotting in order to secure complete surprise, but were helped by heavy mists, which enabled them to cross the river and to reach the foot of the Montello hill, a key position whose capture was vital. RAF planes, immediately diverted from the Asiago front, were instrumental in smashing one of two pontoons over which reinforcements were streaming. Counter attacks by reserve Italian divisions brought the advance to a halt. Another Austrian attack across the Island of Papadopoli in the Piave had little success, but further down the river, a small bridgehead some two and a half miles wide and three miles deep was established, threatening the Italian rear. At the end of the first day each side was satisfied with the position. The Austrians now made the mistake of not following up their advantage, allowing the Italian Commander-in-Chief, General Diaz, assured of the mountain front, to concentrate his reserves on the vital Piave sector. It is true that on the third day the Austrians were able to enlarge their bridgeheads, but now the weather took a hand, converting the temperamental Piave into a torrent and rendering the Austrian positions very precarious. The enemy's communications were cut and he was unable to get his artillery across the river to support the advance. On 19 June the Italians took the offensive, but with little effect. For two more days there was little movement, and on the night of the 21st the Austrians began their withdrawal, which went ahead with little molestation. The great battle had just petered out. What a contrast to the way things were moving on the Western Front, where neither contestant was prepared to let up, whatever the circumstances!

7: THE ASIAGO BATTLE

There was nothing about that camp at Granezza on the morning of 10 June to suggest any imminent change in the routine to which we had become used in the mountains, a mixture of physical discomfort with restful periods in surroundings sometimes almost indescribably beautiful, our minds too full of misgivings and doubts to remain long in repose, all set against a climatic background that mixed English March and May with equivalent inconsistency. Our close-up listening patrols, probing forays and the distant sound of transport behind the Austrian lines had little special significance to us at the time. The public at home, with the aid of a Press never allowed far from army headquarters, had been taught to visualise the troops at the front as ever eager to get at the throats of the hated enemy. As far as we had any other wish than for the end of the war, it was that we should be lucky in avoiding the next large-scale clash. We had seen too much of the inconsequent idiocy of battle to regard it as an experience ever to be sought after. We were all optimistic in hoping to avoid the next battle and indeed almost conditioned not to believe in its imminence until we were brought to realise that it was going to happen.

Although, according to the *Official History*, the onset of the flu epidemic was then receding, the 23rd Division was very short-handed, and on this very day cases were reported in our own battalion. That afternoon we moved up to relieve the Yorkshires in reserve. Our new position was in a camp of bivouacs amidst the pines of a quiet narrow valley behind the Pria dell'Acqua road, an area new to us.

On the two following days it rained almost incessantly and we were at our wits' end to keep dry. Soon the rain was streaming through the sides of our Italian tents and the struggle against the elements was lost. Blankets and everything else had become soaked. We managed at one stage to get a fire alight, but in the drizzle it gave off more smoke than heat. A more disconsolate crowd would be hard to imagine. To cap all this I developed a bad cold, a misfortune to which I had never been particularly subject. No doubt it was something more than a cold, although at the initial stages I did not connect it with the epidemic that was raging. By the second afternoon the storm had abated, although the drips continued to beat a slow tattoo on the canvas sides of our shelter. In my existing condition this was getting on my nerves. My head was thick; I was without energy and no doubt had a touch of the flu. More cases had gone down that morning.

Sitting thus under the weeping canvas, pondering disconsolately over my woes, thinking of home and everything desirable that was out of my reach, I was brought suddenly out of my reveries by the appearance of Sergeant-Major Rhodes, shouting instructions for us to pack up immediately. So unexpected was this turn of events that I almost thought it was a joke, and for a few moments took no notice. But I was quickly brought down to realities and we were soon bustling wearily to move off. Within the hour the company of bedraggled men left to relieve the Durhams in the line. It rained all the way and so a further soaking prepared us for the night post to which we were assigned. The line in that particular sector was held in a somewhat unusual way. During the day we occupied log cabins in the woods at the rear, manning the rock-blasted trenches in front only at night. The line ran down the side of Monte Kaberlaba, crossed a narrow clearing in the valley and disappeared left-wards into a belt of woods, which at that point stretched well out into No Man's Land. Our post on the rising ground to the right had a good field of fire in front, where we were protected by a deep belt of wire, which zigzagged along the whole line, making it pretty secure. This was clearly a key position.

It was cold in the trench that night, and we had the added discomfort of wet clothes slowly drying upon us; certainly not very good treatment for flu! We were not sorry therefore to get back to the hut and to snatch some sleep. In a way we were better off than we had been in the bivouacs. The only snag was the field battery, positioned near-by, which undertook spasmodic shoots throughout the day. Stories were already going round that we were to undertake a stunt against the enemy in a few days, but this seemed a physical impossibility with hundreds going down with the epidemic. We heard that the hospitals behind the lines were already filled to overflowing.

On the evening of 13 June we changed over with another platoon into a large lean-to hut against a considerable wall of rock. This structure, which was divided horizontally into two compartments, made a comfortable billet. Shortly after we had returned to it from the night's patrol, a medical parade was announced and a further half-dozen of the platoon reported sick. I had half a mind to join them, for I was feeling really ill, but two ideas struggled in my mind against doing so: an ingrained dislike of being inquisitioned by the medical people (rooted back in my Somme experience, when trench feet had been allowed to develop by neglect to such an extent that I had become a major casualty) and a strong disinclination to do anything that might be construed as an attempt to evade front line duty. Those others certainly appeared to be no worse than

I was, but experience suggested that they would all soon be returned to us with 'medicine and duty'. Everyone was therefore greatly surprised when word came that they had all been packed off to the rear. During the day we were definitely told that we should take part in a demonstration against the enemy within the next forty-eight hours. I had certainly missed my chance! Ill as I felt, frightened as I should be at again taking part in a battle, I was even more fearful of giving anyone the opportunity to accuse me of slacking. The thing had to be faced. During the afternoon we went to the near-by dump to fetch bombs and small arms ammunition, which we took with us later into the trench, not far away. I was surprised at this and indeed more than a little mystified, for in an attack it would be quite impracticable to take so much weight with us.

We had a good position for the gun but no shelter from the elements. Fortunately the night was clear and bright, though cold. Our guns strafed occasionally, but between their half-hearted outbursts everywhere seemed very still. We had a patrol out and were instructed to keep a keen watch for them. Thus, in the early hours of 15 June 1918, muffled in my greatcoat, I huddled into a corner of the fire-step. I was too cold to do more than doze or twist restlessly in a half-dream. I heard the scrunch of passing feet and a voice talking to the sentries. It sounded miles away, weary and worried. It was Captain Stirling's voice, saying that a gas attack was expected and that we were to keep a sharp look out. This instruction was to be passed on to other sentries. I smiled. This was the sort of nonsense one heard in dreams. A gas attack up here? The Austrians had no guns; they rarely bothered to reply to any provocation. I dozed off again and then woke with a jolt. It was my turn for sentry. I slipped drowsily into the trench. I had not dreamed the captain's words after all: they were repeated now. The wind was right up about something. During our turn we discussed the problem endlessly but could get no reason out of it. Out in front all was quiet, except for an occasional Very light, and we had nothing further to report to our relief.

Orders to stand to had been passed along just before daybreak. Crouching forms were stirring and straightening up on all sides, when something began to happen. Guns were firing out in front, actually out in front! Flashes lit up the hills on the far side of the plateau and a roar of artillery rolled along the entire front. A crescendo of sound, and then the storm burst upon us. Screaming shells rushed to earth amidst the wire, and behind us, or further over in the woods. Lumps of rock were hurled about by the explosions. The trench soon became swathed in a cloud of acrid smoke. My first impulse was to laugh. No guns! Good God! Here was a real slap-up barrage on the Western Front pattern. And soon our own artillery would join in.

Some of the patrol appeared through the haze; there had already been casualties and the officer was missing. Coloured lights went up out of the valley. The enemy's barrage continued unabated, but our own guns remained silent.

Corporal Goffee decided to work up the trench to the right into a quieter and more commanding position. We dodged from bay to bay, now pushing past crouching figures and exchanging an oath here and there, now crouching ourselves as a shell burst nearer than usual. We reached a suitable spot and then discovered that we had left behind some of the spares and magazines. I went back with the corporal. The shells were dropping with awful regularity about the trench; only the hardness of the ground saved us from being buried. But this protective hardness had a terror of its own, as lumps of rock and stone hailed down into the trench. A few tremulous seconds and we had retrieved our stuff and were on the way back, ducking and hesitating at each bend. A particularly fearful blast kept me rooted in a more sheltered corner. A man beside me crouched against the parapet hugging his rifle. In the sickly glare I recognised Bully Peterson. 'This is hell', he muttered, gritting his teeth, 'as bad as Ypres. The bleeding fools to bring us into this without warning.' Although this was a man whom I disliked intensely I could not find a good reason to disagree with him on this occasion. Over my shoulder, as I crouched, I could see the bursts of incendiary shells, and, as I watched, a tremendous flame rose up as some of the trees caught fire. The flames leapt up like gigantic red seas beating against a breakwater and glowed through the gaunt trees which banked up the hillside above us. It was a terrifying but magnificent sight. I rejoined the section breathless but unhurt.

The bombardment continued. Heavy shells streamed over like express trains, to burst in the further recesses of the hills, with a shattering roar which could be heard even above the general bombardment. Cries for stretcher-bearers began to arise on our left, and from time to time word was passed along that some poor devil was wounded or 'had got the knock'. Who would be next?

There were some dug-outs in the trench, deep shafts with openings facing the enemy lines. Why the Italians had constructed them thus, I could not understand. There was one in the very bay we were now occupying. The shells were falling so close to the trench that any cover seemed better than the open trench. Consequently the dug-out began to fill. I found a place in the entrance and was soon lulled into a sense of false security. The flying rock could not hit one there. An officer came dodging along the trench; when he discovered the crowded dug-out he was rightly indignant. He threatened, cajoled and almost cried, but this was no time for him to wield his authority effectively. For my part, I knew he was right, but it felt so secure under the sheltering rock — and there were NCOs among us. We knew that only a direct hit was likely to finish us off there, whereas out in the trench anything might happen.

As it was I spent my time half in and half out of the shelter, according to the intensity of shelling. After a time one gets used to this sort of thing. Reports came up from the valley that were anything but reassuring, and there could be little doubt that our losses were severe and increasing. All the time there was the question in my mind: what was the shelling about? Was this the enemy's accumulated revenge for many pinpricks? It is strange that the truth did not dawn upon us, for none of us took the business really seriously.

A cry of 'Gas!' jerked me out of my musings, and the acrid fumes of a shell-burst close by caused me to imagine that the gas was already upon us. I adjusted my box respirator excitedly, taking more time than was usual on parade and, my companions having done likewise, we crouched round in our weird garb puffing through our rubber mouthpieces and looking like other-world creatures from a novel by H. G. Wells. One man made a sorry mess of adjusting his helmet, got a whiff of gas and had to be taken to higher ground further up the trench to await his chance of getting out. The bombardment, owing no doubt to the use of gas shells, appeared at this juncture to become less severe. No news had come up from the valley since the alarm had sounded and two of us went along to regain contact. The next bay was badly shattered and seemed to be full of gas. We encountered the sergeant-major a little lower down, who signalled that all was ok and waved us back to our position.

The shelling continued, but a little later the 'all clear' having been passed along for gas, we took off our respirators and found the atmosphere bearable. However, the stench of high explosives was so overwhelming that it is doubtful whether we should have detected the presence of gas. We could tell through the smoke that the sun was now up; the bombardment seemed to have been going on for hours.

Through the din, which had certainly lessened, we heard whistle blasts and were puzzled. Suddenly there was a shout from a watcher on the fire-step to our right. 'Stand to! He is coming over!' A chill trickled down my spine. My first impulse was to deny the possibility. The enemy to come all that way across the plateau to attack us: that was an absurd idea!

We grasped our weapons and rushed pell-mell to the fire-step. The barrage was lifting. In front, beyond the belt of wire, a wall of white smoke drifted slowly away. Over to the left, where the tongue of forest stretched forward along the far side of the depression, through the dividing mists, I saw a remarkable sight. An officer in strange uniform on horseback was galloping up and down, marshalling a column of enemy troops into the woods, where they were quickly lost to view. Our trench was manned. The barrage had receded into the woods behind us. A crackle of rifle fire came from among the trees on our left front; a red light shot up in the valley. And still our artillery maintained their extraordinary silence. The rifle fire developed into an unbroken rattle and it was obvious that the enemy were working their way through the woods towards the front line. Rifle shots and occasional Lewis gun bursts were directed from our trench but we were at a disadvantage, despite our fine view along the flank. In front the ground sloped away some fifty yards or so on this side of the wire, and movements further down the gulley were hidden from us. The edge of the woods, where the enemy was still massing, was too far away for effective fire. After one or two experimental bursts with the gun, Corporal Goffee decided to conserve ammunition. I borrowed a rifle and took one or two long shots. Thus, nearly two years after I first went to France, I had my first shot at the enemy. On the Western Front, even in an offensive, one rarely saw him until he was a prisoner.

The thrill of fear experienced at the announcement of the attack had soon subsided and now, standing in the shelter of our rock-hewn trench with a part of the battlefield stretched before me, I felt a curiosity that mastered all other feelings. I was now witnessing a battle from a viewpoint that a press correspondent might have envied. The occasional shell-burst behind our parados had little significance after the recent ordeal, and at this stage our job of holding the trench did not seem likely to be a difficult one.

Meanwhile things were getting lively in the woods. More coloured lights went up — despairingly it seemed — and the hollow crash of bombs punctuated the rattle of musketry. A stiff fight was being put up by our advance posts. Then I saw khaki figures running back, followed closely by grey lines of the enemy, moving more methodically, while reinforcements continued to stream across the plateau into the end of the wood now in the enemy's rear. The combatants drew parallel with us and well within rifle-shot, but we were unable to shoot as it was difficult to distinguish friend from foe in the melee. Our only task for the time being was to keep a look out over the slope in front.

It was then, I think, that we began to realise that things were not going very favourably and that our own position was being threatened. We had no artillery support; the woods in front were crammed with Austrians. If only we could have dropped a barrage there at this juncture. But we did not. The troops in the wood below came to grips in earnest, but all details were blocked out by the clouds of smoke that curled among the trees. I saw the flash of cold steel and the stabbing flames from rifles fired at close quarters. The wood was being fiercely contested by the men of the 48th Division, but the enemy's onslaught was too heavy and the defenders continued to fall back, leaving our flank in the air.

At this moment the battle seemed to come to a stop. Then, with a thunderous report, the wood literally burst into flames and a tremendous cloud of muck and fume shot into the air. The dump from which we had drawn our stores had blown up. At the time this was so closely synchronised with the flow of battle that we concluded that our withdrawing troops had fired the dump and that the enemy had suffered a momentary check.

If so, this certainly did not last long. Enemy troops penetrated further to the rear and bullets began to flick over the back of our trench. We had the unwelcome feeling of being surrounded, though of course this was an exaggeration. I thought of the small forces behind us, of the close proximity of the plains, and the possibility of disaster loomed in my mind. Coloured lights now went up from behind, signals no doubt to the enemy artillery for them to move their barrage further over, while, out in front, groups of the enemy continued to manoeuvre unmolested except by distant and therefore very chancy rifle fire.

Crack! Crack! Shots came from the rear across the back of the trench as the enemy enfiladed us. The third act of the show was about to unfold itself. Enemy troops were spotted in the gully below us and the whole trench opened out with a roar.

But the bulging ground sheltered the attackers until they got close to the wires. Then we were astounded to see a small party appear right up at the wire in the dip straight in front of the company. They were apparently in dead ground as far as our left flank was concerned, for no fire was directed against them from the lower end of the trench. The attackers, appearing to enjoy charmed lives, then put something into the wire and ran back quickly. The bomb or torpedo exploded with considerable concussion, blowing a complete section of the wire into the air and clearing a passage through the belt. It was an amazing feat. A party of the enemy then rushed the gap under cover of the dense smoke from the explosion, and were in the trench in a matter of seconds. Almost simultaneously a stooping figure appeared above the brow about twenty-five yards in front of us, an enemy soldier bowed down with the weight of some infernal contrivance, a flame-thrower as we subsequently discovered. The trench belched fire from end to end and the poor brave devil fell forward on the skyline riddled by dozens of bullets. With one's knowledge of the possibilities of this fiery weapon, who can say how near to success this lone attacker had come? His companions, if he had any, failed to come into view, though we continued to keep a wary eye in that direction.

Our position was getting precarious. From below came the noise of bursting bombs and rifle shots fired between the close sides of the trench. All we could see were the black shapes of the missiles as they were lobbed from one bay to the next. The enemy were establishing themselves. We aligned our gun along the trench, but there was little we could do without the risk of hitting our own people. Bullets kept hitting the parapet, causing us to bob up and down like marionettes. The remnants of the company began to flow up the trench past us and we had visions of a general withdrawal over the hill to our right. A member of the left platoon came up, blackened from head to foot by a close-bursting bomb and almost demented with the concussion. He named pals trapped and wounded, before he collapsed on the fire-step and the stretcher-bearers took a hand. Others came by, half-shellshocked and demoralised. The enemy were gaining ground. Corporal Harkins came into the bay, looking for spare ammunition. He sent a man up the trench over the brow to beg, borrow or steal supplies from our neighbours. The NCOs were at their wits' end. Our gun was useless in this sort of engagement.

Then the miracle happened. At this critical moment leadership began to operate. Captain Stirling, looking taller and more gaunt than ever, appeared on the parados and called for volunteers to counterattack the captured section. Electrified by his example and glad at seeing a possible solution to a grisly dilemma, the men in our part of the trench, raising a shout, began to clamber up after him. We were all carried away by a real wave of enthusiasm, and the section would have abandoned the gun to a man if level-headed Corporal Goffee had not ordered us back to our position to support the forward movement.

The attacking party was quickly marshalled into line by the captain and the sergeant-major, who had also come on to the scene. These two tall figures, waving the line forward, set off in the forefront of the attack, which was in effect a move to storm our own positions. It was a magnificent movement and a glorious sight. The two leaders, slightly ahead, striding forward and swinging like catapults as they hurled their Mills bombs, followed by the improvised line of riflemen with bayonets fixed, pivoted from the back of the trench and converged in a half-circle upon the unobstructed rear of the captured section. Their bombs were soon bursting about the position. Our invaders did not await the impact. Feeling, no doubt, that too much could be asked of mere flesh and blood, they left the trench in disorder and fled towards the woods, while our men disappeared into the trench with a cheer, which was taken up by all of us. Hitherto I had seen no one fall and our casualties must have so far been very light. But now tragedy intervened. Elated by their success, the excited attackers leapt up on to the parapet with the obvious intention of following the retreating enemy. This was a foolish and unnecessary thing to do, only to be accounted for by the uncontrolled excitement of the moment. Already the Austrians had got far and the baffled pursuers began to snipe at them with their rifles. Enemy troops occupying the surrounding woods immediately opened fire, and many of our company fell never to rise again. A few survivors scattered back into the trench as best they could. The company's position was again intact. From our vantage point we had been little more than spectators of this action, since our men were between us and the enemy most of the time. Fire from our end of the trench had therefore been desultory. But it was all over in a matter of seconds.

This seemed to be the turning point of the battle. The Austrians, we heard, had penetrated well back into the lines of the 48th Division, whose troops were now holding two switch lines, against which the enemy was failing to make any further progress. Even our own battalion headquarter staffs in the rear had taken part in the turning movement. As far as we were immediately concerned the situation now seemed to settle down, while the enemy, to signify his ill-success, began to bombard us with one of his batteries. The bursting shells, in conjunction with the constant sniping across the trench, left us with little reason for complacency.

From all reports our casualties had been severe. Both the junior officers, including our platoon commander, who had never been under fire before, had been killed; Corporal Harkins, whose happy smile and permanent good temper had made him the company's favourite NCO, lay dead out on the parapet, killed in the counterattack, in which Sergeant-Major Rhodes was among the wounded. A section of our Number 5 Platoon had been buried in a neighbouring dug-out under an immense mass of stone. Of the eight or nine victims, whose bodies were subsequently, after laborious efforts, dug out one by one, one man by some miraculous chance was found still alive and was taken to the dressing station in the hope that something might still be done for him. By the irony of fate the dead were all well-built robust chaps whereas the survivor was the most weakly member of the group, a youth who had generally been considered 'not quite all there'. Many of those left in the trench had received bad bruises from flying stones, while others showed signs of shell-shock or gas. We had lost Hardcastle with a shrapnel wound and one of our attached men with a touch of gas, but the section had actually fared better than most. I was unharmed, as usual, and all traces of my illness had gone, routed no doubt by the morning's excitements. We were all very tired and dirty and, now that the first shock of a battle had passed, were already congratulating ourselves on survival, although the operation was far from finished.

While our company was again reduced to less than half strength the rest of the battalion had also suffered heavily. A whole platoon in the supporting company had been wiped out by a heavy shell, which registered a direct hit on their dug-out,

159

while a patrol of one of the other companies, which had engaged the enemy in the early stages, had been badly cut up.

The next few hours were spent in clearing up the debris in the trench and preparing for further eventualities. Parties of the enemy could be seen retreating across the plateau, burdened with wounded and material. The attack on the left was no longer developing and news came in that, under pressure from the reinforcing battalions, the enemy were beginning to withdraw from their hard-won positions. In the woods the terrific onslaught of the first attacks had given way to desultory sniping.

A young officer from 'A' Company was sent in to assist Captain Stirling, who had been left on his own. The captain made a tour of the positions, looking very fatigued and worried. When he came into our bay he evinced great surprise and shook me by the hand, saying that he had thought he had seen me lying dead on the top of the trench. I was amazed at this incident. I do not know which of my feelings was more powerful at the time: a pleasurable surprise at his unexpected solicitude or a heartfelt gratitude that the captain's vision had proved incorrect!

Meanwhile our artillery still remained quiet. It was understandable that the bombardment had broken all the wires strung between the trees but we could not make out why they had not fired on the SOS lines. When things had slowed down an artillery officer, accompanied by his NCO with a coil of wire and a field telephone, came into the trench and selected our bay as the most suitable for his Observation Point. They set about getting the guns aligned on new targets. This was not easy as the battery was somewhere behind the hill and it was difficult to avoid the tops of the trees without firing too wide. The first shots cut things very fine and pitched but a little way in front of the trench. At last the officer appeared to be satisfied and, at a further command, the battery opened out in earnest. The first shells fell among the retreating enemy groups, scattering them in all directions. The enemy were collecting around Coda, a sort of quarry, which we could see clearly from the trench and which now made a splendid target.

I watched this display in a detached sort of way, noting each successful shot with a revengeful satisfaction. Those moving figures, looking like flies in the distance, some already wounded and getting away from the battle as best they could, were not human beings to me at that moment. They were just targets for tearing metal. We who had suffered so many times from the same terror stood there and applauded every successful shot. That is what war had become in a scientific age — an impersonal mathematical destruction.

During the afternoon an enemy battery, firing somewhere over to our left, caught the trench in enfilade, while rifle bullets continued to crack into the parados behind. But we were fortunate and suffered no further casualties. After nightfall reinforcements came in. The remnants of 'B' Company were collected together and led out of the devastated line. Our guide gave us to understand that care was necessary, since the enemy still held posts at the rear within a few hundred yards. If we took the wrong turning we might blunder back into the zone of fire. The situation was still unstable. We got clear, however, with nothing worse than a few snipers' bullets fired haphazardly in the dusk, but as the guide led us up the hill the line straggled out and some of us lost touch. Thus, I passed the night with a few others, weak and cold, stranded on a strange hillside, longing ardently for the dawn but at the same time fearing that at that hour another barrage similar to yesterday's might discover us in that very exposed situation. Fatigued as I was, I did not want to die just then. The chill mountain air flowed through my close-wrapped greatcoat like cold water and seemed to take triumphant possession of my body as I lay amidst the boulders. The hours dragged away slowly, and in the darkness I imagined the dead of yesterday beckoning to me. The irony of dying of exposure after escaping that storm of steel struck me forcibly, and I struggled to my feet with the idea of making a fight for it. As I stood there swaying I saw in the distant sky the first faint signs of a new day. The world that had trembled beneath an avalanche of metal the morning before now lay quiet with death. This very stillness intensified my terror and I looked furtively towards the northern sky for those warning flashes that never came. A new day — thank God for a new day!

In the daylight we soon discovered the company's resting place, by the roadside among the pines where we had been billeted a couple of months before, not in huts this time but in a narrow tunnel running deep into the hillside, lined with wire stretcher beds in various stages of disrepair. The sap was horribly wet, the water streaming down through the rocks, for the ground had not yet drained from the recent rains. But it was as safe as any such place could be.

Now we were collected here, the sad gaps in the company were fully apparent. Captain Stirling was a changed man, his demeanour towards us now quite different. We were 'his' company, what was left of us. Soon after our arrival he told us that he was proud of his command, though I do not think at the time we were very clear about the reason for this. Everything was still so mixed up. However, we were grateful for his consideration, for he did everything possible to make the place comfortable. In such circumstances the intention as much as the deed makes all the difference in keeping up morale.

We heard that the enemy had failed all along this mountain front and that in fact our troops were occupying positions out towards Canove, which had previously been in Austrian hands. The advance posts of the 48th Division out in the woods had been taken by surprise. Some of our men had been caught half-dressed, an unheard-of liberty in such a position. The barrage must have missed them entirely, otherwise they would have had plenty to think about. It was said that our kitchen dixies, recaptured from the enemy, had been used as latrines, a disgusting gesture that failed to touch our sense of humour.

The enemy's losses, we felt, must have been heavy both in casualties and prisoners. We saw some of the latter passing the sap on their way back, and were struck by their fine physique and deportment. They must have been picked troops; we looked like a band of decrepits beside them. This was our reaction at the time, but the truth no doubt was that they did not have their hearts in the fight.

8: UNCERTAIN INTERLUDE

We were now entering a period of indecision, during which our movements would be even more unsettled than usual. The future seemed as vague and threatening as ever, although events were already shaping the final act, which would break upon us suddenly and surpass our every expectation. Not that our expectations were very high at this stage.

While the events described in the historical note were taking place we were still in the mountains, licking our wounds, unaware for some time of what had been happening on other parts of the front. We knew there had been a great victory but were far from sure that the enemy would leave it at that. One of the things we did not know was that almost immediately General Foch, who was about to assume supreme co-ordinating powers over the Allied Armies, was pressing General Diaz to stage an offensive in the mountains, at a time when the Germans were committing their reserves in a number of offensives on the Western Front. This plan was supported by Lord Cavan, subject to sufficient troops being available but, as the *Official History* makes clear, a good deal of shilly-shallying went on and little was done.

Up in the mountains we hung about in support for a day or two, taking cover when our artillery chose to bombard the Austrian positions. This they did with a will and the enemy had not yet recovered sufficiently to reply. On 17 June I find myself writing:

Today the rain has swished down unceasingly through the melancholy forests and had it not been for the occasional 'strafes' by our guns — now wide awake after the event — it

164

would have been difficult to realise the presence of an enemy in these dismal altitudes.

In our discussions of the recent battle we were unanimous over the intensity of the Austrian barrage, which, while it lasted, had been as heavy as the shelling on the Flanders front. At about the same time we were both enlightened and annoyed by the loudly-voiced opinion of an English-speaking Italian engineer, who derided the view that there had been anything exceptional about the enemy bombardment of 15 June. Asiago, he said, was the Italian Ypres 'only much worse'. We felt that a weekend on the Salient would have changed his mind. From his safe hillside dug-out, happenings on two such diverse fronts were bound to look very different.

Moreover there was plenty of evidence of the weight of the recent bombardment in the back areas. In the hillsides we had seen chasms that would have hidden a small house, while everywhere among the trees there were new shell holes, some as far back as Granezza and beyond, where the shells had actually been falling over the edge of the plateau. But the interesting point about all this was that many of these shell holes were in virgin territory previously untouched by artillery fire, a clear indication that Asiago, despite its long battle experience, had not been subjected to such intense pounding before. Tales from the rear told how some Italian gunners had abandoned the heavies for which the Austrians were probing, feeling no doubt that the time had come to take a little trip down to the plains. This impulse had been scotched by the prompt action of our military traffic controls — at the point of the revolver.

We went back to Pria dell'Acqua in reserve on 18 June, but were back in the line to relieve the Durhams three days later. All the time, there were patrollings and stand-tos for raids by other units, and everyone was kept on tenterhooks. In our new position we were actually in support bivouacs in the woods, furnishing patrols in No Man's Land at night, and working parties during the day. The nights were brilliantly moonlit, so that the white walls of buildings quite a long way off stood out clearly against the dark background of the pines. Everywhere was so quiet, yet there was an expectant note in the hush. Surely something was about to happen! But nothing did on our first night. The following night we stood-to while a neighbouring battalion made a raid on the enemy positions. Our artillery opened out impressively as if by clockwork. Thirty-two prisoners and a machine gun were brought back by the raiders. At this very time four men from the company went home on leave, and there was much rejoicing in the ranks.

An order from army headquarters spoke in praise of the infantry rifle fire during the Austrian attack. Evidence of this was to be seen in No Man's Land, which was cluttered with equipment and the bodies of Austrian dead. The corpses of men from five different divisions were identified on our front, including those of Germans sent out to help their allies. On the patrols there had been much souvenir hunting, for little respect was paid to the dead and the attempts at burial had been very half-hearted. As the nights passed the stench that polluted the crystal clear atmosphere became almost unbearable. One poor fellow lay in a grotesque attitude with the lower parts of his body showing immodestly where he had dragged at his clothing in pain — a fat burly man who would have looked at home serving in a butcher's shop in Vienna or Budapest, where perhaps a loving wife and children at that very moment waited anxiously for news. He had gained a petty notoriety in death: for everyone was asking whether we had seen the big fellow displaying his most private parts and advising those who had not, with suitable verbal embroideries, not to miss a comical sight. Our only excuse was that we had nothing better to laugh at.

At stand-to on 24 June Captain Stirling came round the positions to read out orders from headquarters on the importance of discipline in the trenches. The brass hats had to have their little jokes! We were not sorry, therefore, on the following day to receive instructions to pack up and move out. But it was a much depleted and dispirited company that took the road to Granezza once more. There were too many gaps in our ranks. After a battle a unit looks strange, and it was long since we had been like this, a scratched and chipped thing until new material arrived to fill the vacancies.

On reaching Granezza we did our best to cheer ourselves up, which was certainly helped by the provision of a picture show at the divisional theatre. We heard that an impending counterattack by our forces, which had been rumoured during the last few days, was off, and naturally we were pleased. The following morning we enjoyed the luxury of a visit to the army baths, now also installed on the mountain plateau at brigade headquarters just above the settlement.

Almost immediately we were led off in full marching order down the steep stone-strewn paths towards the foothills — a trying form of locomotion with such heavy loads on our backs, though the direction helped to lighten the burden. For billets we were assigned to a barn, not too clean but a luxury after our nights on the plateau. The first event was kit inspection, as a result of which I was ordered to company stores to draw a brand new suit, in different shades of khaki, it is true, but this was a sufficiently rare event to give me a good deal of pleasure. Such things just happened to us. We could initiate little ourselves.

During the first morning our surroundings were blotted out by a heavy blanket of rain — a common occurrence in these luscious hills, which gain so much from the moisture. After the storm the surrounding scene took on a new magnificence, which even our bored military eyes could not ignore. Here on the foothills all was green and fruitful, in contrast to the barren ruggedness of the heights above and the dry summery plains below. In a house beneath the billet I saw a truly amazing sight. The good people kept silk-worms — it might be more correct to say the fruitful silk-worms kept the good people — for in stacked wooden trays, that occupied practically all spare living space from floor to ceiling, the silk-worms ate their picked mulberry leaves or made yellow cocoons. Everywhere there were silk-worms and cocoons, on the walls as well as in the trays; everywhere loose threads of gossamer silk strayed, and above it all there was the persistent noise of multitudes eating. In their parlour, thus invested by the welcome hordes of caterpillars, the Italian proprietors made the most of the little living space left to them. I never saw anything like this again, no doubt because we rarely had an opportunity to see what went on inside those peasant homes.

This was a time of inspections and reorganisation. Promotions to fill the gaps among the NCOs were virtually hawked round, and there were many refusals. As usual some accepted responsibility who were quite lacking in the right qualities, but other advancements were well merited. Our Corporal Goffee at last obtained his sergeant's stripe and, while we were glad for his sake, we were sorry that he now had to leave the section; the gap was filled by bringing back Lance-Corporal Westgarth to take charge of the gun team. Some members of recent drafts were among the promotees. To all this I adopted the part of spectator. My own standards for leadership were high, too high for me modestly to imagine that I could match up to them. Of course few others did, but that, I considered, was their funeral — as it too frequently was! I evinced an extreme lack of appreciation of what might well be my own true interest. But I could not be promoted and remain Number One, and I preferred to continue to carry my revolver. At this time we went to the brigade school to select a physical jerks team for a forthcoming competition. I am a little surprised to discover that I was one of the members of the company team, but I have no note of what happened later, nor do I remember whether the competition ever took place. There was always something inconsequential about the way plans worked out in the army.

We were understandably disappointed when, on the last day of June, orders were issued for us to get ready to climb the mountains again, pack mules being assigned for transport of the Lewis guns. When we moved off the next day we kept to the main highway, which zigzagged up from the foothills. If this meant a much longer march, the going proved much easier and we reached a small village just under the ridge late in the afternoon. We stayed there in bivouacs on the hillside for the next three nights but, finding the night air cool after our brief sojourn below, some of us discovered unofficial shelter in a disused cattle pen. We had plenty of time to contemplate the scene below — a quilt of infinite greens and blues threaded with white ribbons along which an occasional dispatch rider indicated how the route played hide and seek around the curving mountainsides. On the second day the brigadier-general looked in, for once ceremony being dispensed with.

On 4 July we relieved the Yorkshires in the front line in a sector away to the right of Monte Kaberlaba, where the Notts and Derbys had sustained one of the major Austrian thrusts on the 15th. Here the enemy had made a narrow penetration, only to be ejected later in the day. It was still unmistakeably a battlefield, littered with the debris of war and so different in appearance from the many other quiet forest fringes through which our line meandered. We were soon scrounging for souvenirs among the litter. I salvaged a short blood-stained Austrian bayonet, which I managed to hold on to throughout the rest of the campaign and have before me on the desk at this moment. I remember subjecting it to a good deal of cleansing at the time but the stain still shows.

In the parados of the deep rock-hewn trench we occupied timber-roofed shelters, which were cosy enough as cover from the elements but a real trap in case of shelling, since they constituted weakening bites out of the main trench. Just here the trees thinned out, but were probably still sufficient to hide the position. In front there was a good belt of wire and, a couple of hundred yards beyond, a small tree-clad hillock standing out like an island on the plateau. This was occupied by one of our advance posts in close contact with the enemy. We were told that we were close enough here for mortar fire, an unusual position on this part of the front. We had two sections of only four men each to hold the trench and man a small post in the wire as a sort of liaison with the advance post out in front.

At times things got quite hectic, with mutual shelling by both artilleries. At night there was considerable activity between the advance posts. This was certainly the liveliest sector we had yet occupied in Italy — a bit like old times. At stand-to on our second morning the French carried out a successful raid away to our right, bringing back a number of prisoners. The enemy retaliated by shelling our positions. On 7 July we heard that our artillery had been ordered to stop shooting for a day or two.

Probably some sort of reorganisation was being undertaken. The enemy must have known, or read more into the silence than he needed to, for we were subjected to a continual strafe all day, making us keep our heads down. Shells fell within a few feet of the trench, but short of a direct hit the rock was too hard for them to cause much damage. Anyway, we were fortunate, and moreover discovered a deep sap in the hillside to our left, which would have afforded good cover had the shelling become more intense.

However, during our six days in this trench, there were plenty of quieter moments. During the day a refreshing breeze blew under the pines, where bright sunbeams pierced the shadows, making the tree vaults as impressive as the interior of a towering cathedral. At night a thousand fireflies flitted about the edges of the wood and the world assumed a new beauty until a distant gun flash from behind the Austrian positions momentarily eclipsed nature's minute lanterns.

These were the times when we talked of the past and yearned for our distant homes. It was on 9 July that the first batch of Tyneside papers reached the battalion through the post, filled with gleeful reports of the way the Northumberland Fusiliers had acquitted themselves in the recent battle. In one there was a vivid drawing of members of the regiment jumping out of their trench in face of hordes of the enemy shouting 'They shall not pass' — a journalist's typical interpretation of reality. Of course it was not like that at all. Yet we were not altogether displeased at our brief moment of notoriety. We heard to that our battalion had been mentioned in the Italian communiques.

On 10 July our 10th Battalion took over the line while we went into the reserve position on the hill-top behind. Here we were assigned to a trench which was quite devoid of shelter and decided to look elsewhere for cover from the elements. I found a place in a hut occupied by one of the other platoons. This sort of thing was only possible because of our depleted numbers.

Our job during the next ten days was to provide working parties, either repairing the paths during the day or out wiring in front at night. Regular hours were imposed, the day party packing up at 4 pm sharp, but I avoided much of this by taking over the job of mess orderly, while at the same time keeping the gun ready for action. During this period at least three heavy raids were undertaken by the French and ourselves, on each occasion accompanied by a full-scale artillery bombardment. The pyrotechnic effects were magnificent and a number of prisoners were brought in, but it is doubtful whether these affairs served any better purpose than to increase the casualties on both sides. From time to time the woods were shelled and I found my nerves on edge. This was accentuated when a chance shell fell near a shanty just down the track, occupied by headquarters people. Two tradesmen were killed and others wounded. Normally they would have considered themselves as safe as houses.

Papers from home at this time brought news that the Western Front had quietened down somewhat, but the accompanying maps showed that extraordinarily large bites had been made by the Germans into our trench system, and with our knowledge of what that had hitherto meant we saw little reason for optimism. There was news of the great efforts being made to hasten the American reinforcements. The traditional laughing Tommies were, despite everything, still spoiling for the fight! It is true that we did manage to laugh quite a lot, but for very different reasons. Our moods alternated between states of boredom and occasional interludes of hilarity. Over the nearby battery, whose firing often caused us concern, there was a line of camouflage. In Blighty, we knew, they had plenty of camouflage of a different sort and we were not amused. No one knew what was really happening, least of all we who were in the midst of it.

On 15 July drill-khaki uniforms were issued to us and, as if to mark the event, hot summer weather descended upon the mountains. The days became sweltering and even the rum ration became excessive, for no one wanted that sort of boost under the new conditions. We paraded for pay and I received the princely sum of fifty Italian lire.

It was thus with great joy that we learned on 20 July that the division was being relieved and that we were to go back again to the bivouacs on the edge of the mountains. It was a glorious sight to look down upon the plains once again, to feel the prison walls receding a little, with the sight of an occasional civilian face to remind us of the freedom below. Only those who have been temporarily cut off from the ordinary world know just what that means. We were fed, we were clothed, we were lodged, everything was arranged for us; but when the opportunity came to spend a few lire on some small thing that we may not particularly have wanted, we experienced a slight touch of treasured liberty.

The next day brought us down into the summer heat of a camp in the foothills near Fara. We spent most of the time bathing in a cool stream running alongside the camp, where the waters were shaded by a row of birch trees. Explorers discovered, a little further afield, a reach of the stream which had been dammed to form a swimming pool and thither we trooped garbed in shirt and towel, presenting no doubt a weird sight to the stolid countryfolk toiling under their black umbrellas. Articles of underclothing washed in the sparkling waters were dry in a few minutes. Sun lovers that we were we soon found ourselves seeking out the shade in self-defence.

All too short was our stay in this demi-paradise, for on 23 July, at 6pm in the cool of the evening, we were ready again to march away. At that very hour thunderclouds gathered over the mountains and broke swiftly upon us. But the military machine, once its schedules have been settled, pays small heed to the elements. All the usual evolutions were carried out, culminating in a general salute with hundreds of bayonets flashing in the reflected light of the storm, while lightning played above the trees. The rain poured down as we set off on our march, but the storm cleared as quickly as it had come and before the first halt our new drill uniforms were beginning to give up their moisture. After two more evening marches we reached the pleasant little township of Arzignano, situated among the farthest spurs of the Alpine foothills. The heights slope up steeply on the northern edge of the village, crowned on the nearer summit by the usual relic of mediaeval power, the castle, which was clearly visible from our billet. I hoped when I first saw it that I might one day find my way up to it, but at that stage of the war my natural inclination to make such peregrinations had reached a low ebb and I have to admit that I never did. We occupied an empty factory, which made a spacious and clean billet and overlooked a wide open space that might have been used as a fair ground. On the far side of this a soldiers' club had already been established, with facilities for reading and writing, while the town had its own miniature theatre. The shops of course were soon doing a roaring trade in the small necessaries on which the troops were wont to spend so much of their spare cash, and I remember a special line of solid brilliantine, in fancy jars of a type one then expected to find only in the luxury shops of large cities.

We were soon hard at work cleaning up, for it was made clear to us that a period of spit and polish had arrived. Particularly difficult to remove were the stains from our leather equipment, which had run into the new uniforms. But we were aided by a long open lobby in the billet, into which the sun streamed and which provided a wonderful drying room. We also had trouble with the long puggaree which had to be wrapped round our newly issued pith helmets. This consisted of yards and yards of light khaki cloth, whose proper arrangement was quite an art. We were fortunate to have a few Indian veterans in the company, whose services were in great demand.

Parades were fixed for 6 to 7 am, 8 to 10 am and 5 to 6 pm, with a long siesta in the afternoon. In this we emulated the local people, who kept off the streets when the sun was at its fiercest, though I cannot say that we always followed their example to the letter. Outside, the sunlight in the afternoon was so intense that all colour gradations seemed to disappear from the scene and the walls of the buildings to coalesce in a glaring whiteness. Within, apart from the vivid patches of sunlight coming through open vents and windows, everywhere was shadowed in dense blackness. Our meals were also switched: we had tea at midday and the inevitable stew, now even less palatable than ever, was served in the evening. Lime juice appeared on the ration list.

Our afternoons could have been the best time for reading and quiet contemplation — or sleep. But the card players were soon in their element again, playing not only the inevitable pontoon but also 'housey'. Some idiot had brought a set of the latter back from sick-leave and the billet soon echoed to the raucous shouts which I thought we had left behind long ago at

Etaples. Unfortunately the noisy and the quiet groups were about equally divided, so there was little we could do about it.

Otherwise normal army routines soon filled in the time. Firing on the range, inspection of kit, arms practice, church parade on Sunday, and even some lectures. In the evenings the band of the Yorkshires sometimes played in the square or gave a concert in the soldiers' home, and were much applauded. There were impromptu concerts at which the most awful turns were generously spared the bird, and The Dumps put on a new revue which they called 'Camouflage'. But this was a different matter. The evening Doniger and I went along to the miniature theatre to see them the audience were uproariously appreciative. Many were the digs at the brass hats, and these never failed to raise the roof. It did us good to get rid of some of our bottled resentment in this way. One day I had a sudden cold, which surprised me in that wonderful weather, but it must have disappeared as quickly as it came for I did not mention it again.

The news from France continued to be disappointing. The papers were foreshadowing the turn of the tide, but we had little faith in their prognostications at this stage of the war. We were certainly becoming better served with news, for I made a note that the continental edition of the *Daily Mail* could now be purchased in the area. News had been received through personal sources that the battalions withdrawn from our front earlier in the year had been involved in the German advances and had suffered heavy casualties.

On 25 July, according to the *Official History*, the American 332nd Infantry Regiment, which had recently arrived in France with their 83rd Division, was sent to Italy. Certainly there were rumours about this time of the arrival of American troops but I did not make a note of this and do not remember when it was. In any case the inflow was certainly exaggerated and shipping difficulties prevented any further American units being spared for Italy.

There was an interesting event on 30 July, when the battalion paraded with great ceremony to witness the presentation of the Victoria Cross to 2nd Lieutenant Youll[8] of 'C' Company, whose exploit at the Battle of Asiago has already been mentioned. This was a great honour to the battalion, and indeed to the regiment as a whole, as the Northumberland Fusiliers, despite its many battalions, had previously earned only two of these medals since the outbreak of the war. Ardent Northumbrians sought to excuse this by alleging that the Fighting Fifth had on some occasion earned the displeasure of Queen Victoria and was thenceforth disqualified from receiving her most coveted award. Whatever truth there may

---

[8] The official citation reads: 'John Scott Youll, Second Lieut., 11th Battn. Northumberland Fusiliers. For most conspicuous bravery and devotion to duty during enemy attacks when in command of a patrol, which came under the hostile barrage. Sending his men back to safety, he remained to observe the situation. Unable subsequently to rejoin his company, Second Lieut. Youll reported to a neighbouring unit and when the enemy attacked he maintained his position with several men of different units until the troops on his left had given way and an enemy machine-gun had opened fire from behind him. He rushed the gun, and, having killed most of the team, opened fire on the enemy with the captured gun, inflicting heavy casualties. Then, finding that the enemy had gained a footing in a portion of the front line, he organised and carried out with a few men three separate counter-attacks. On each occasion he drove back the enemy, but was unable to maintain his position by reason of reverse fire. Throughout the fighting his complete disregard of personal safety and very gallant leading set a magnificent example to all.' He was killed in action on 27 October 1918 at the crossing of the Piave at the age of 20.

have been in this, the explanation is interesting as the sort of myth that passed among us. A tale was told of our harum-scarum hero — of whose bravery there could have been not the slightest doubt — that on one occasion when making his rounds he had found a dug-out converted into a miniature Monte Carlo, and, instead of putting an immediate end to such a grave deviation from army regulations, he had at once entered into the betting himself! This tale may well have been apocryphal but it certainly hit off the character of the man as it was assessed in the ranks. He was a very unorthodox holder of His Majesty's commission.

Many other honours were conferred. The colonel and Captain Stirling both received the Distinguished Service Order and the absent Sergeant-Major Rhodes a bar to his Military Medal. A windy runner on the company staff, who had been pressed into the job owing to heavy casualties among the regular members, well earned his MM, and also one of our stretcher-bearers, who, however, rather lost his companions' sympathy, by himself asserting that this was a poor reward for what he had done. Lack of modesty was never popular even among the more hard-headed, somewhat mercenary types. Of course there was the usual quota of awards, which had surely been allocated as part of the ration. The general wound up the proceedings by quoting from the report of the relieving division commending the state of the trenches and the good work done during our tour. Those working parties were really necessary after all!

Our ten days sojourn at Arzignano came to an end on 3 August, on the morning of which the colonel chose to make a personal kit inspection. In conformity with regulations we laid out our kits round the billet like children playing shops. The great man appeared, severe and impenetrable. His eagle eye immediately spotted a grave deficiency: my cap badge was missing. In fact I had lent it to a member of the headquarters guard, by request. A barrage of wrath descended upon me. Did I not know the regulations? I began hesitatingly to offer my explanation, half-expecting someone else to clear up such a minor misunderstanding. My utterance was cut short by a stentorian 'Take his name!' from the regimental sergeant-major, the inevitable threat of punishment. I felt no less of a worm when matters were satisfactorily straightened out afterwards. It was this sort of childish pettiness that made the army so unattractive to anyone with the least sensitiveness or independence of mind. This episode was followed by a short lecture on the history of the regiment. Yet there was no enthusiasm when, during the same afternoon, orders came to leave our pleasant billet and to march some seven miles up into the Berici Hills.

As it turned out the change was not all loss: we were in bivouacs up on the hills and the surrounding panorama was magnificent. The sunshine continued, but during the heat of the day there was a tempering breeze, which made the atmosphere very pleasant. We spent the time mostly in gun practice and manoeuvres, mainly to induct new members of the team into their new duties. Our first full day in these rural surroundings was 4 August and my twenty-first birthday, which I passed quietly, not at the time worrying very much about another lost memory; there could be no celebrations though I have no doubt my mother remembered.

We soon found that life here had its darker side. In the mornings women and girls, apparently of the gypsy type, came to the camp from the surrounding villages with baskets of fruit and chocolate, which they endeavoured, not unsuccessfully, to sell at exorbitant prices. They were generally driven off by an irate orderly sergeant, but not before unauthorised purchases had been made. Money always burned in our pockets. In the process hands reached out from under the bivouac in a clutch at a stockingless leg, which was invariably evaded by a vigorous kick at the canvas. They were certainly hardened females but the sights they saw in a camp at that hour must have been an education to all but the most experienced.

At this time, encouraged both by opportunity and by reasonably good rations, sex had become the most prominent topic of conversation, and it seemed from all reports that the company's Don Juans were in good fortune. At least one of the many farmhouses which studded the surrounding countryside had been converted by its enterprising inhabitants into a thriving 'red lamp' and, judging from reports, which were freely disseminated with injudicious detail, the organisation was very business-like. The women no doubt found this a much more lucrative business than toiling in the fields or breaking stones on the roads for the government. By combining business with pleasure they carried on while their husbands and sweethearts, away at the front, were offering their lives for the beloved fatherland.

To me the glory of the surrounding scene was a continuing revelation throughout our lazy interlude. One day, after a heavy thunderstorm, the evening air was marvellously sweet and clear and for once the haze that usually shrouded the plains to the south had dispersed. There the distant Apennines stood out clearly, a blue fringe along the horizon, while further westward the first serried spurs of the Maritime Alps were clearly discernible. Never had I seen such a glorious view. To the north the whole range of the Carnatic Alps and the heights of the Trentino unfolded themselves before me, rising in a natural wall from the plains. Over there were the Asiago and Tomba heights, with the mole-like Montello crouching low to the right and the Astico and Brenta valleys making gaps in between. The towering peaks above were still distinctly white, while the green billowy foothills looked insignificant at their base. Normally the sun scorched down upon a haze that seemed to lap like a sea up to the hills. But on the day in question this panorama of natural magnificence had one little warning touch. Over in the direction of the Grappa group, high up towards the summits, I could see the pinpoint sparks of bursting shells. There the line clung precariously to the mountains and the battle went on ceaselessly.

On 10 August I was a member of a small party given the day off to visit the horse show at Trissino. We were late in starting, having first been instructed to draw new drill uniforms at the store. No doubt this was one of those official arrangements to ensure that there was a sufficient sprinkling of 'other ranks' at the essentially aristocratic amusement. As it turned out our motor lorry did not arrive until after the morning events had ended. Trissino was a delightful little hamlet, set amidst lush greenery under a hill studded with picturesque white-walled villas and dark green tree clumps. The place teemed with brass hats in full regalia and officers in their smartest rig-out. It all looked very 'pukka'. We decided not to await the afternoon performance but returned to the Quartermaster's Stores, where we stayed the night and helped with the loading in the morning, preparatory to rejoining the battalion, which had now taken up billets on the outskirts of Arzignano.

Our few days sojourn there were signalised by a complete change in the military outlook. Special communiques were read out on parade on 12 August, announcing that at last the tide had turned in France. This was the first we heard of the Allies' successful counter-blow, launched on the 8th of the month. To me at the time it merely seemed that a very painful interlude had very properly been brought to a close. But it was more than that, for history was witnessing the beginning of the end.

On Tuesday the little township held its market. The roads leading into it were crammed with the jogging transport of the peasants bringing in their produce from the outlying villages. To witness their leisurely progress, their placid faces, their business-like stock, was to realise they had something much more important in life to be concerned with than the gigantic struggle taking place under their very noses, with the ever-present possibility that, in a sudden swoop from those neighbourly mountains, bloody war might at any time carry all before it. Yet there could be few among the families represented there that had not made its contribution to the firing line, and the predominance of black in the dresses of the women may not have been entirely attributable to custom, even though they were habitually so fond of drab attire. During the midday rest, when practically all the peasantry and townsfolk had taken shelter somewhere and the sun seemed to be having it all its own way, I walked into the town and made some purchases, mainly at the canteen, where I laid in a good store of chocolate and, feeling in a flourishing condition, I purchased a ticket for The Dumps on the following night, when a bumper house was to enjoy their new revue 'Something Doing'. That same day serge uniforms were re-issued and we knew that we were shortly leaving for the mountains again.

On 18 August, at the end of three days' march, we arrived back at the camp in the foothills. This was a red-letter day for me, for my name was taken for leave, which meant going home in about seven or eight weeks. I could hardly believe my good fortune, though I had known this to be imminent, and was almost speechless with joy. This was the sort of thing that happened to one only in dreams. I prayed that time might now take wing and fate continue to be kind. During those last few days, I noted, our rations had been unusually generous and there was more food than we could eat.

On the morrow we reached the reserve position after a stiff climb. Passing over boulder-strewn fields which formed a ledge a short way from the top, we saw a large herd of plump brown cows grazing on the scant grass and a well-built peasant girl, under whose charge they were, knitting quietly as she sat upon a large stone, possibly the last outpost of the civilian world below. She paid no attention to the toiling files as they curled past her along the stony path, too exhausted to evince the usual reaction to the presence of a skirt.

Up here on the few flat spots which fringe the road, huts and bivouacs had been established. There was a Church Army hut not far away and, rather nearer, the headquarters of a balloon unit, which was sufficiently rare on that front to attract notice. The balloon itself hung in the sky above us seeming hardly high enough to observe beyond the wall of rock and stone which rose steeply on the far side of the road. It was a wild spot, given some enchantment by the widespread scene far below us. We were on the left divisional front, which we had occupied for a short spell when we first came to the mountains in the spring.

On the following day I was chosen to go up with an advance party under an officer to reconnoitre our new positions and the concentration areas near the line. The expedition was uneventful enough, for the front was quiet, though we saw further evidence of the June battle, but our return journey rather made up for that. We were fortunate to jump an Army Service Corps lorry, an Italian Fiat, which the British driver handled with all the flair of a native. The price of such impetuosity was everywhere in evidence in the abandoned and usually shattered vehicles frequently seen on the steep hillsides below the road. Our route skirted the Astico Valley, running along a perilously winding edge with a sheer drop of many hundreds of feet, past the line of low posts which fringed the outer lip, into an immense green chasm trenching into the vast mountain barrier. The driver, pleased no doubt at having such an opportunity to show off, put the machine through its paces, skirting those fearful bends at top speed near the outer edge with but inches to spare. He knew his job, which was as well for us. These few spare infantrymen, so proud of the risks they took, were being put decisively in their place. And we could say nothing while the show was on. I saw ghostly visions of all those derelict cars which I have mentioned. That my reactions were shared by my companions was made manifest when, on our alighting, the platoon sergeant murmured laconically, 'The bastard!'

For over a week we stayed there, poised between plain and mountain, carrying out the usual parades or making a trip into the support position to repair the mule tracks. At this time the platoons were reorganised into three sections instead of four. The weather remained hot, a good excuse to laze on the hillside contemplating the magnificent scene around us. On the far side of the valley, in the shadow of the distant slope, a large white splotch denoted the town of Schio, which guards the route into the mountains, while further up the valley where the sides came closer, a *teleferiche* transported shells from the plains below. These cable railways were much in use for raising heavy weights to the heights, and occasionally venturesome soldiers made unauthorised use of them as a convenient short cut.

On 27 August we took over the front line positions in the

woods to the left of Monte Kaberlaba, below the trench we had occupied on 15 June. On the way in we halted by a breastwork, which marked the furthest enemy advance on that occasion and which was still littered about with abandoned enemy equipment and arms. There, a good mile back from the front, the state of the ground still indicated the titanic struggle which had culminated at that spot as the enemy tide, rolling strongly towards the edge of the mountains, had been stubbornly brought to a halt.

We were comfortably situated in our new position, occupying a string of posts with fairly good observation over the plateau. During the previous night another battalion had carried out a large raid on the enemy, according to reports, bringing back sixty prisoners and suffering few casualties. This must have been the raid undertaken by the 10th Duke of Wellington's, which is mentioned in the *Official History* as having taken place near Vaister. Eighty men were killed and sixty-five captured in this raid at a cost of fifty-six casualties, and it is indicative of the sort of warfare which had been going on all along the British and French fronts, although it was to slacken off during September. We no doubt escaped the experience because of our mauling in the main attack.

On 1 September the battalion took a single Austrian prisoner. He was reported to have been in the army only two months, of which he had spent fifteen days in the line. Now we thought him a very lucky dog!

On the following day further good news came from France — too good, we thought, to be true. To show the somewhat inconsequential nature of the warfare up in the mountains, I picked up near our gun post a pass permitting a corporal and eleven men of the Royal Field Artillery to go into No Man's Land. Our section leader, Westgarth, having been sent out to run in the 7th Division sports, I found myself in command for the first time, and I must say, despite all my convictions to the contrary, I felt quite important at this small enhancement and encountered no difficulties in doing what was wanted. Looking back over the years I can see now that I was much too modest about my own capacities. The competition was not really stiff and I suffered from a surfeit of diffidence, which could have been counter-balanced by a more confident type of education.

The Durhams took over from us on 4 September, when we staggered up over the mountain barrier with full pack and blanket on our backs to go into reserve near Cesuna. Here we were to undertake guard duties and working parties, mainly on the roads and mountain paths, which were always in need of repair. Many new things seemed to be changing the tenor of our military life at that juncture. Even the value of the lira went up, to 2s 9d for five lire, as a result, it was said, of a recent American loan to Italy. Not that the explanation would have made much sense at the time, for there were no students of economics in our company. Another day proxy voting papers were distributed for the general election then in progress at home. We were out of touch with politics, though most stuck to their old labels, as current arguments usually proved. Lloyd George's Coalition seemed, on what little information we had, to be the best choice.

At this time the boxing competitions brought a new interest into our fives, for it happened that the ring for the semi-finals had been set up in our valley. This bleak, rock-strewn furrow in the hills, sparsely clad with pine and fir and often wreathed in mist, had become on the evening of 9 September, the scene of great human activity and even greater excitement. Below our straggling row of huts, sheltered by the stone supporting walls of the road, there were scattered in the dip a few green patches, our erstwhile parade grounds, gashed here and there by the shells that occasionally screamed over the mountain barrier. On these grassy islets a professional job had been made of the ring, now thronged around on its four sides by spectators from many regiments, who found suitable viewpoints on the sloping terraces. Here was a picture for the war artist, which, as far as I know, was never painted, the sort of thing one had seen in prints of eighteenth-century England. A band was playing popular selections to create a tone for the occasion. I was no judge of boxing, but many of the matches that evening seemed to me very good, and, judging from the encouragement and applause of the audience, indeed, they were. To me the light sparring matches gave much more pleasure than the sheer slogging displays, in which brawn rather than science decided the issue. But the match of the evening was between a sergeant from our battalion headquarters and a member of the Machine Gun Corps. Our man had come to us only a few months before with a somewhat unsavoury reputation, which included wearing medal ribbons for which he had no claim, but whether true or not he had lost no time in making himself as unpopular as could be. For a time he had acted as provost sergeant, a post that requires the greatest tact under the best conditions if unpopularity is to be avoided. Thus our loyalty was divided: we wanted our man to win, even though as a man we thought little of him. The sergeant stepped into the ring flamboyantly, victory already in his hands, but the business-like demeanour of the machine gunner, a well set-up youngster, promised at least a good show. The sergeant's first lightning attack seemed to miss fire, his opponent evaded him elusively and appeared to be unshakeable. Within that first half-minute the mood of the crowd changed unmistakably. We sensed the possibility of our man being licked. Our man, he might be, but an unpopular bully he also was, and thenceforth every blow by his opponent was received with a cheer. The latter must have been surprised to receive so much applause for routine hitting, especially from strangers. Honours were about even at the end of the first round; then there came a change and our man began to alternate between reckless attacks and undecided defensiveness. The machine gunner remained unruffled, now and again putting in a nasty jab, as if to promise more in good time. By the end of the fourth round the sergeant's face was covered with blood, while he had begun to beat the air with his gloves. In the fifth round the end came: our man fell like a log under a clean straight punch and was counted out. The victor received a great ovation. Never was there a more popular win. Nevertheless, it has to be admitted that the sergeant had fought gamely, and admiration for his plucky exhibition overcame the antipathy of the onlookers as his seconds helped him out of the ring. A few nights later the finals were fought. Further down the valley they had set up a travelling cinema with an open-air screen, but I must confess that I was too lazy to walk along to enjoy this unusual *alfresco* treat.

A large draft joined us on 12 September, bringing the battalion up to full strength again. They were mostly youngsters of twenty years or less and seemed young to me, who was but a year their senior. They were, however, younger in experience and had not yet seen death at close quarters, an experience which ages any human being. Most of them no doubt were conscripts, but this did not have any perceptible effect upon their demeanour. How they felt about it all is difficult to say, for newcomers in such a situation are not inclined to unmask their inner doubts. We must have appeared as peculiar to them as my predecessors had appeared to me when I had first joined the 7th Northumberland Fusiliers on the Somme in September 1916. As this account will show, they were in time to experience a big battle and to prove that they could take it.

We went back into the front line again on 17 September for what was to be our last battle experience on the mountain front. This was the very day arranged, according to the *Official History*, for the 23rd Division to be relieved to go to France, but as we shall see, the scheme was not to be fulfilled.

We now occupied a post in a wood at the end of a trench, half dug, half breastwork, which crept round a steep bank from the rear position. We were under observation during the day and thus were only able to keep night sentries in the post itself. The people we relieved told us that the sector had been very lively ever since the Austrian attack, and this was soon to be borne out. Our other platoons held strong points somewhere above us and over to the left, where they were under continuous shell-fire during our stay. The front in the mountains was so varied that we never knew what to expect. Certainly on this occasion there were some quite unusual factors. For example, we had a dug-out, which was well hidden amongst the tree roots, but too flimsy for protection, and full of rats. These unwelcome beasts made a continuous noise during the night, squeaking and scampering behind the wooden supports. Out in front our view was unobstructed by the trees of the wood and but lightly protected by a few half-hearted strands of wire. The field of fire was poor and it was reported that the enemy kept a patrol out in front at night. If he had decided to take a few prisoners we should have been a most suitable objective.

Our first day was quiet enough, but at stand-to the enemy subjected us to one of the most business-like bombardments we had experienced from him, except during the major attack.

We really expected something to happen. Shells fell all round the dug-out and in the woods out in front. During the demonstration Westgarth, myself and the Number Two stood by the gun, which was trained forward in anticipation of a target that failed to appear. As a measure of caution, to minimise casualties, the rest of the team were ordered to spread out in the trench, but again we came through without a scratch, though I think more by luck than by judgement. It was warm while it lasted, leaving us in the usual state of jumpiness, which seemed to get more pronounced as the war lengthened.

We then went back into the woods in reserve for a few days, during which time there was a good deal of shelling among the trees, and again we were kept on tenterhooks. On the night of 24 September we took shelter while our artillery put up a full-scale bombardment, in support, it was said, of an Italian attack on another sector. Then news came that the Italians were digging new gun pits further down the valley, and there was some interchange of information with them. One, who could speak English, frankly told us that we were not very popular with his compatriots — our presence had lengthened the war for them! Such attitudes may well have been more indicative of the possibilities of the situation than much of what was recorded in the official accounts on both sides.

We had heard that the Italians were coming up to relieve us. On 26 September one of their divisions arrived, and we went back to the huts at the corner where the road leads out above the Astico valley. The relieving troops were very different from the rag-tag and bobtail to which we had become accustomed. They were a fine body of men with plenty of war experience behind them, most of them wearing battle ribbons. We did not know at the time, but we had seen the last of mountain warfare.

On 29 September we descended the mountain wall in lorries and, following a night march through the foothills with bands playing, we found ourselves in an airy barn with the lovely summer weather still continuing. Two matters on 2 October were found worthy of a note in my diary: I had a raging toothache and the CO read out to the battalion particulars of a new educational scheme which was being introduced — an excellent idea, but in my opinion, at least two years too late. By 6 October we were back in Arzignano again, a move which we much approved, billeted in a large store-room in a big country house standing in its own grounds just outside the town. We heard that day that Bulgaria, the first of Germany's allies to collapse, had capitulated on 30 September.

Already the presence of troops in the area was being signalised by the usual civilian reactions. One of the more pleasing of these was the way the children thronged round for sweets, mimicking our uncouth Anglo-Saxon expletives. They copied the songs very well indeed and unless one listened very carefully it was far from obvious that they did not understand a word of what they were mimicking. A song which they produced particularly well was one of our favourites at the time, which ran something like the following:

Good-bye-e, don't sigh-e
Wipe a tear, baby dear, from your eye-e
Though it's hard to part, I know
I'd be tickled to death to go
Good-bye-e, don't sigh-e
There's a silver lining in the sky-e
Bon soir, old thing, cheerio, chin, chin
Na poo, toodle-oo; good-bye-e.

The children's total impression was right, even if most of the words were quite unintelligible.

A rainy spell gave the authorities an opportunity to launch the educational scheme, which was to operate on a voluntary basis. The customers paraded at the sergeants' mess to undergo a preliminary test, graded 'simple' and 'medium'. I took the latter, which was simple enough in all conscience, but I was appalled by my current lack of knowledge. Schooling seemed so far behind, the continuity had been broken and the war seemed to have been going on since childhood. This was a dead loss in our lives, which many were never subsequently to retrieve.

The medium test, which had to be completed in one hour, consisted of:

(i) A short essay, with choice of subject.
(ii) A few lines to be written on each of five subjects: geographical and general.
(iii) Four simple arithmetical problems: simple and compound interest, etc.

It interests me to record that I proposed to take up the classes in shorthand and languages, but as far as I remember very little came of all this. Great events were pending.

As I sat contentedly in our half-deserted billet on the afternoon of 11 October, turning over in my mind the idea of visiting the canteen, a messenger of evil entered. He had heard, he announced, addressing no one in particular, that all leave had been cancelled. I affected not to be interested, but an awful sickness gripped my heart, so awful that I can remember that moment vividly today. In my life my capacity to hate has never been acute, but I hated the guts of that man. I tried to discount his news as just another rumour; but this would not work. That sort of thing always turned out to be true. Anyway,

I knew it was true. I was among the next two or three on the company list and it could have been any time now. Just my luck!

It was Sunday, 13 October 1918. Reveille was sounded at lam for the battalion to stand to from 4.30am. Already the day before the evil tidings had been officially confirmed. All leave was stopped. The proposed field scheme was cancelled. My spirits, unconsciously buoyed up by the glorious prospect of soon going home, had dropped to zero. On that day we awaited instructions, which did not come until after church parade at 11 am. We were to move off on the morrow. The drums were beating. The final curtain was about to be raised. Already the numbers of many of those worthy men, my companions, who had long survived the holocaust, were engraved on the scroll of fate. All but the most unimaginative at that eleventh hour could hear the murmur of a funeral march in their souls.

HISTORICAL NOTE: THE END IN SIGHT

In France the situation had now radically changed. The Germans had delivered what was to prove their last massive attack in a dual blow, known as the Battle of Champagne and the Second Battle of the Marne, offering a further serious threat to Paris. Foch's well-timed counter-blow sent Ludendorff over to the defensive. Haig, with full French co-operation, planned a further counter-blow at Amiens on 8 August, and the Germans were treated to their own medicine. Thenceforward the battle flowed towards the frontiers and suddenly, indeed unexpectedly to most, the end came in sight. By the beginning of October the German and Austrian governments were approaching President Wilson for an armistice, but the Allies were in no mood to compromise.

A comprehensive plan had been drawn up by the Allies in Italy for a series of attacks, both in the mountains and across the Piave river, and 24 October chosen for its launching. On the mountain front a strong attack by the Italians in the Monte Grappa sector, after some initial successes, was brought to a halt by stout Austrian resistance. The main crossing of the Piave had been assigned to the Italian Eighth Army on the left, the Anglo-Italian Tenth Army in the centre, and the Italian Third Army on the right to the sea. The operation was to be launched with the capture of the Grave di Papadopoli, a large shingly island in the Piave. This was successfully undertaken by the British 7th Division on 24 October, but an immediate follow up, involving a crossing of the river from the island to establish a bridgehead, was delayed by the weather. As the text shows, the actual attack was not launched until 27 October. This was carried forward by the two British divisions, the 23rd on the left and the 7th on the right, without the support of the Italian forces on either side of them, which were unable to get across. The attacking divisions had to organise the defence of the open flanks, where they could have been fatally vulnerable had the Austrians been on their toes. Yet at the end of the day all objectives had been taken.

On the far left of the river front, troops of the French 23rd Division (forming part of the Italian Twelfth Army, which was commanded by the French General Graziani) had secured a bridgehead and repelled several counterattacks, but they had not been assigned a major role at this stage. The Italian Eighth Army, however, had been less successful, its bridgehead having proved too small to permit the necessary bridging operations. Thus the Italian Eighth Army, cast to play the principal part in the offensive, had been unable to move. By the flow of events Lord Cavan's Tenth Army took its place as the spearhead of the attack, which in three days was to drive the Austrians beyond the Monticano and to open the way to victory along the entire front.

9: THE CROSSING OF THE PIAVE

It was raining hard when we left Arzignano on 14 October, heavily burdened with a special issue of winter underwear in our packs and a rolled blanket. We covered seventeen kilometres in all, passing through the ancient town of Vicenza on the way to the railhead, where we entrained for an unknown destination. Marching through Vicenza, with its tattered hoardings and many-shuttered houses, we saw little to indicate its peacetime serenity and architectural distinction. All around us in the cities of the Lombardian plain there was art and culture, the glory of human magic hidden away in dark cellars. It was not till many years after that I realised how near I had been in those days to some of the most beautiful products of human vision and skill.

But who bothered about that sort of thing when one's very survival was at issue? The train left at 6.30 that evening, landing us at Mestre in the small hours of the morning, with the rain still pouring down. Here we were packed into a leaking factory nearby, and those who happened to find themselves on a spot where no water was dripping were fortunate. Our blankets were saturated by the morning. Yet, despite all that, I slept soundly, as is the way of youth, and joined in the general grouse at being bundled out first thing to continue the journey. After a good deal of shilly-shallying we ended up in a farm just outside Mirano, fairly comfortably housed but much too crowded.

When the rain had cleared the atmosphere became crystal-like and invigorating. A trip to the town during the first evening of our stay introduced us to an attractive place. The country had a different, richer appearance but this impression was general and it was not easy to account for the difference. The buildings were certainly more attractive, with a good deal of external decoration, and there was a richness in the foliage, palms flourishing here and there. On looking at my pocket map I was surprised to discover that we were in the neighbourhood of Venice, on the far right of the Italian line where the Piave entered the sea. We were still in the dark as to the plan behind the move. It was now being freely rumoured that the idea was to mislead the enemy by making large-scale troop movements behind the lines. The officers looked worried and Captain Stirling had been like a bear with a sore head for some days.

The rain continued on and off. We paraded between showers, getting more and more fed up. I noted at the time that there was no sign of leave being resumed, which showed what was gnawing within me and the unrealistic nature of my assessment of the events then unfolding.

We marched off again in the evening of 19 October, stopping for a night in a barn somewhere and marching on through Treviso, the communications centre behind the Piave positions. No sooner had we arrived than the whole battalion, now equipped in battle order, marched off for a new destination. The mystery of our movement was not disclosed until we reached a stream running swiftly between high banks. We filed along the tow-path to a number of flat-bottom boats, moored under the charge of Italian boatmen (many of whom, I learned, were gondoliers from Venice). In a very short time the whole battalion had been transported across the stream and back in accordance with detailed instructions. The unusual-looking craft were skilfully manoeuvred across the swiftly flowing current by a sort of broadside movement. We were told to get in and out quickly, and how to keep low both to ballast the craft and to avoid enemy bullets. Despite the rather unstable conditions as the boat swayed across the turbulent stream, the whole operation went according to plan and without the least mishap. For once the army got on with a job without messing about.

On the way back all kinds of reasons for this sudden manoeuvre were discussed. We had been informed that the practice had been carried out in case of a sudden enemy attack, but we were not to be taken in by that. There were other much more likely rumours. The most favoured story was that the Italians were making an attack and that we had been brought up in support. I cannot think why we really thought we should be given such a secondary role, unless it was that we realised that two British divisions did not go very far and that, in any case, it would be only right that the Italians should take the leading part in liberating their country. We ought to have known better, but there was a strong feeling about that the war would be won without anything being done in Italy and that it was a mistake to sacrifice fives unnecessarily. This could have been a doubtful assumption, but in any case the idea of saving human lives at the expense of a little glory did not enter into the minds of the General Staff in that war, as the accounts of statesmen and war-leaders were abundantly to show when the time for the inquest arrived.

We had hardly got back and nicely settled into our billet when, as the result of the owner informing the authorities that there had recently been cases of measles in her house, we had to move again to another building. We had our own views about the truth of this allegation and a hope was openly endorsed that a stray Austrian projectile might find its target amidst the disease-stricken brickwork! After tea, pay parade somewhat mitigated our annoyance. On the afternoon of 22 October we were marched off again through Treviso — which showed widespread signs of enemy bombardment both by long distance gunfire and air attack — to about four kilometres beyond, where we were dumped in a field while a taking-over party went in search of billets. All this messing about and indecision, without the least explanation, annoyed us very much. Indeed, it was a poor prelude to what lay immediately ahead. After two hours wait, by which time night had fallen, the guides returned and we were taken to a large four-square country house, in which Number 6 Platoon occupied the attic. That night enemy planes came over, presumably concentrating upon Treviso. Our anti-aircraft fire was intense, spent shrapnel raining down on the slates above our heads. As I lay in my blanket I could see out through one of the low windows, which came down to the level of the floor. The whole surrounding area was ablaze with flashes, while enemy planes chugged overhead. One or two bombs fell in the immediate neighbourhood, causing the house to reverberate with the explosions, but we made no move to seek shelter elsewhere. This would have been difficult in any case, but our nonchalance was due, I think, to sheer fatigue and a sense of impotence. The Austrians must have known that troop movements were going on in the area.

On the following morning orders came for the battalion to stand to. There was a hurried consultation between the captain and the NCOs who, on their return, informed us that we were ordered to make an attack immediately — across the Piave. The officers, they said, were very pessimistic about the scheme, even Captain Stirling, whom hitherto nothing had seemed to daunt. He had remarked to his batman that he would much sooner go home on leave!

All this came as a great shock to us. Why so, I find it difficult to understand today in the light of the previous ten days' movements. The point was that we were now getting heartening news from France and hopes were rising that the war would soon end without our having to take any further active part. It was a case of wilfully failing to face the facts.

During the afternoon of 23 October a party of our officers and NCOs went into the Italian-held trenches along the river to reconnoitre. They were garbed in Italian helmets and capes to mislead any enemy observer who might spot them. Their report was that the front was comparatively quiet though some lively counter-battery firing was in progress. But it was the roaring Piave that worried us.

We moved off later, arriving in a field somewhere near the front early in the morning and sleeping the rest of the cold night in the open. That day was passed in making the final preparations — issue of bombs and small arms ammunition; the cleaning of guns. The usual reinforcements squad were told to attach themselves to the transport, and I was glad that both Tom Ireland and Isaac Doniger were among this lucky band. But I was upset at not being given a turn with the reinforcements. When I looked round the company, which was a woeful spectacle on that day, I was unable to discover anyone else who had had as long a continuous frontline attachment as myself, without break for one reason or another. Though there were a few with longer service in the battalion, there was no one else who had not missed a stunt since I joined them in May of the previous year. I felt that my run of fortune had been phenomenal and could not possibly extend any further. Surely my number was up this time! I took the very unmilitary step of pointing this out to the machine gun sergeant, and it is characteristic of the change in attitude then widely in evidence that he listened sympathetically — it happened that he was not coming in himself — and made some representations on my behalf. But the outcome was a foregone conclusion. Experienced Lewis gunners could not be spared, particularly as the company's complement of guns had recently been doubled. This was true enough and I should have known better. It was cowardly even to try, but the roar of the torrent struck additional terror in my soul.

During the night a party of expert swimmers had gone forward to look for suitable fording places. They had failed to cross one stream and a swimmer had been washed away.

The plan of attack was now explained to us in greater detail. The Italians were to attack on our right, the 7th and 23rd British Divisions forming the left wing of the advance. We had the honour of being the left company of the left battalion at the very end of the line. After crossing the river — here said to be about two miles wide — we should have an exposed flank until an Italian army, crossing further north, towards the Montello, swung down to meet us some distance behind the Austrian positions, with the result, if successful, of cutting off a considerable Austrian army. Thus the Eighth Italian Army was to take the principal part in the battle. (Our 48th Division was remaining in the mountains). The usual flippancies about taking the red, the white, and the blue hues were conspicuous by their absence. In fact, our officers were a real collection of Job's comforters on this occasion — not that we required much prompting, with the river ahead roaring exultantly in our ears.

We moved off after tea on the evening of 25 October, proceeding single file alongside a transport-crowded road through a shattered village reminiscent of the Western Front. There was little incident. We did pass one section of the road which the enemy had recently shelled with his heavies but the journey in was quiet enough, except for the damnable roar of the river. Our assembly point was in an open field behind a row of dug-outs along a low dyke which formed the riverbank. The field kitchens came up to serve a meal, which promised to be the last supper for many. We waited while the darkness thickened and a desultory shelling beat time to the ever-surging waters, now just ahead. The officers stood apart, or occasionally glided from group to group. Our low murmuring conversation turned to previous stunts, to the possibilities of peace, but not to those thoughts of home that filled all our hearts.

Then word came that the streams were swollen and impassable; for the moment we were reprieved and must have felt the same sort of relief as a condemned man in a similar situation. Back again in our field we obtained bivouacs and set them up all round the perimeter to evade observation. Who could describe the sheer enjoyment of the sleep we had never expected! In the morning orders were given to pack up, as the attack was cancelled. The news was received with joyous excitement as we set about light-heartedly to move off. While these preparations were in progress enemy planes came over and machined-gunned one of our observation balloons, whose occupants came down safely in parachutes. The Allied artillery caught one of the attackers.

We marched off singing, but had not gone far when a halt was called. After a brief consultation between the officers at the head of the column, we were turned back and told that the attack was to take place after all. It need hardly be said that we were angry at having our hopes thus unnecessarily raised and our depression was deeper than ever.

In the bivouacs we spent another night, which was broken by intense artillery fire from both sides and the rattle of rifle and machine guns in the distance. Many shells burst in the surrounding fields but there was no point in leaving our bivouacs and, as it happened, we suffered no casualties. We heard that troops of the 7th Division had attacked and captured an island occupied by the enemy, preparatory to the main attack, which would now be launched early next morning.

On the evening of 26 October we went again to the assembly point, where supper of porridge and tea was served. The night was dark and noisy. Some enemy shells screamed over the embankment ahead and burst perilously close to our halting place. On all sides one could sense the movement of troops and transports. Our bombardment, we had been told, would open out at 11.30 pm and we were eager to get well forward before the curtain went up. In my view it was silly to give the enemy such an early warning that something big was afoot, but of course some action was necessary to soften up the Austrian positions and particularly to cut the wire in front of their trenches.

The hour of 11 was approaching before the guides came to lead us into our trenches, where we loitered for some time. In retrospect it is clear why there was all this apparent indecision and waiting about. We were virtually queueing up for our turn at the crossing points, but we did not know that at the time. An enemy battery began to fire at the trench and the shooting was sufficiently accurate to cause us to crouch low behind the sandbagged parapet. This was a good start! It seemed that the Austrians were not going to take matters lying down. In such situations one invariably gave one's opponent the credit for more foresight than he usually had. I was torn between a fear of the close bursting shells and apprehension about the intensified barrage which our gunfire must inevitably draw upon us. The minutes ticked away. Why couldn't they get a move on? At 11.20 pm the enemy battery ceased firing, and both lines lay quiet under a dark, star-speckled sky. Only the river continued to roar, drowning all minor sounds. We began to move again, rounding a corner of the trench into a straight piece along the riverbank, presumably our front line.

Our guide mounted the parapet, and it happened that the time was just 11.30 pm. The guns behind us opened out as we began to rush across the shingle. There was no resounding crash as in Flanders, but an increasing roar as the batteries took up the chorus miles away both to our left and to our right. Thousands of gun flashes coalesced to form a continuous blaze of light along the bank behind us and, so open was the riverbed, that the spectacle assumed a magnificence unknown to the puny participant in the more concentrated bombardments of other fronts. Breathless and agitated as I was, I could not suppress a sensation of sheer wonder, a sort of involuntary appreciation at taking part in such a tremendous operation, coupled with a feeling of complete insignificance under the mighty man-made storm. Our shells screamed overhead in an unceasing stream, seeming, though we could not see them, to roof the skies above us before bursting amidst the enemy positions on the distant bank, so far away that as they beat the ground it sounded like a roll of many drums, while each separate burst sparked up momentarily in the darkness out in front. This was something new in my battle experience and that night is one of the rare moments of my life still pictorially engraved in my memory.

As we crossed a well-constructed footbridge spanning the first raging stream, the enemy's reply began to arrive. Shells crashed into the shingle or exploded in the air above, but without the usual warning screams, which were masked by the combined din of our own artillery and the even more insistent noise of the exultant waters now all around us. A cloud of smoke from the batteries behind us swept across the riverbed and I felt as though I had been hurled into the very centre of Pandemonium. I heard a scream near at hand and saw a member of the platoon spin round and reel back into the murk, hit somewhere in the side or arm. We had suffered our first casualty and no doubt most of us were wondering who would be next.

Now we came to the second stream, which presented a much more formidable barrier than the first. We could discern the dark waters swirling by in the dusk. A couple of small boats were moored to the bank, under the charge of Italian pontooneers. They sat nonchalantly smoking cigarettes, apparently ignoring the bursting enemy shells in the vicinity. I felt a great admiration for their sang-froid and did not envy them their job. They had to stay in that exposed place, while we at any rate would keep moving with some hope of occasional cover. They were the guardians of the pontoon, which now appeared in silhouette a few yards downstream. A string of small boats had been thrown across the river in such a way that the powerful current tended to force them closer together, and they supported a planked gangway, which was roped across their gunwales. Over this bridge the assault troops had to pass, regulated by an Italian boatman to ensure that the structure should not become over-loaded at any point. We were to proceed at three-pace intervals. I saw a steel-helmeted figure mount the bridge and stride slowly forward; and another, and another. The gangway stood some feet above the water and in the darkness seemed to be hung high in the air. The flaming horizon beyond threw the dark figures into relief, while shrapnel shells stabbed the darkness above. I was thrilled by the heroic sight, despite the intense fear that was gripping me. I knew I had to traverse those swaying planks with the rest and the idea was not a pleasant one. Slowly the file tramped on, away into the glare. Now it was the man before me. The Italian raised his finger. I gripped the Lewis gun more firmly to my shoulder, gritting my teeth and thinking, 'I musn't let this foreigner see that I am frightened'. He puffed his cigarette unconcernedly. 'One. Two. Three.' He nodded. I went forward and seemed to have to step up high into the air to reach the gangway. I felt terribly exposed up there. The planks of the bridge were absurdly narrow. The bridge swayed. The dark waters swirled and foamed below between the boats. A shrapnel shell burst venomously above. Slowly, now, no panic! Tramp, tramp, tramp. The bridge swayed rhythmically. A shell screaming into the waters alongside threw up a column of water, which splashed across the planks. I wanted to run; but no, we kept our paces, proceeding as if by clockwork. And then I saw the opposite bank looming out of the darkness. A shell burst somewhere behind; the bridge trembled and there was a sound of rending woodwork. I ran and jumped clear, sinking to my knees on the welcoming shingle. Word passed that the file behind had lost touch, but after a very brief halt the rear began to close up, and it was obvious that the damage had not been serious. If the Austrians had been successful in smashing the bridge the events of the following day might have been very different. Huddled in a group on the bank under guard were a number of enemy prisoners, captured no doubt in the previous night's operations. They were awaiting an opportunity to cross back to safety.

We moved forward from the riverbank, and were ordered to spread out and lie down. This we did without loss of time and almost simultaneously the enemy intensified his bombardment of the captured island. The shells rained around us, each burst throwing out a thousand sparks as the shrapnel drove against the loose stones. Hereabouts the ground was absolutely flat, affording not the least bit of cover. There was nothing to do but dig in with our entrenching tools and gradually I scraped up a low barrier of loose stones to protect my head. Having something to occupy oneself made all the difference, however little use the scooped-up heap of stones might prove. On that ground the shells had a particularly terrifying impact: they struck the stones like immense flails, as the force of each explosion blew fiercely over us. A few yards to my left another figure lay as though dead. His face was towards me, and I recognised a member of the recent draft who was for the first time under fire; he seemed agonised with fear. I shouted to him to copy me in using his entrenching tool but he seemed too paralysed to respond. Cries for stretcher-bearers came from behind. An officer ran across bending low, instructing us to hang on and not to move till orders were given. They could not risk a panic at that juncture. Orders did come at last and, the enemy barrage having somewhat lifted, we filed away through some bushes on the edge of the island. I saw one figure that did not rise with the rest of us and guessed that there must be other similar victims in the darkness.

Our next stopping place was at the back of a captured trench, which we were instructed on no account to occupy. And so we lay along the old enemy parapet while the bombardment continued. Most of the stuff was going further back but now and again the enemy dropped his barrage round the old positions. This was not a very sensible place to occupy, but on the other hand the shelling seemed to be pretty general, the whole riverbed constituting a somewhat indiscriminate target. We had more losses, agonised shouts rising from time to time, followed by the coming and going of the stretcher-bearers, whose efforts could not be too highly praised. Nevertheless, I cannot think our losses were very serious, and it was a good thing that the enemy was too uncertain of the situation to be able to concentrate his guns on really worthwhile targets.

At last we were ordered forward again. We found ourselves on the edge of the main torrent, which now had to be forded, for we had left the bridged streams behind. In front of us swirled an ominous black current which, with the enemy barrage now well in the rear, we had the unmixed blessing of contemplating without other fears intervening. A shallow ridge had been discovered just here, where it was expected a crossing could be safely effected. I was already frozen from our previous inactivity, for it was a very cold night. The guides started forward into the darkness; warned by previous experience, we linked together in continuous chains of four or five and scrambled after them. The cold waters swept up round my body. I gasped as my heart seemed to stand still and I felt my feet going from under me. I had to hold the gun well above the waters. We strove vigorously in the torrent, which now came up to our shoulders. Then the worst was past, and the bed sloped up to the shore, on to which I scrambled, frozen and breathless from the struggle. Drenched and bedraggled, we had little of the appearance of an assaulting force at that moment. Immediately we set about helping those who were following on. It was soon apparent that not all had been so fortunate. There was a fairly heavy toll of men missing, of rifles, machine guns and ammunition lost in the waters.

Among the missing was one of the well-known old hands of Number 8 Platoon Lewis gun team, an amiable fellow of very short stature, who, despite the strenuous efforts of his companions, had disappeared in the swirling torrent. He could of course have survived, but the chances seemed pretty slim.

Our main bombardment continued, over-shadowing the puny enemy reply, but all seemed quiet here except for the torrent. We were out of things for the time being. We did not know how near we might be to the enemy positions, and it seemed that the scrunching of many feet on the shingle was bound to disclose our presence. The jumping-off line having been decided upon by the officers in accordance with the orders for battle, we were told to settle down and wait quietly until dawn. Although our movement up till now had appeared to occupy a considerable time, it was early yet, with several hours to daybreak.

Behind us there was the slight rise of the island we had crossed; in front everything looked flat and open. The shelling slowly died down and both lines became still. I scooped out a hollow in the ground, laid my gun carefully aside and tried to get some sleep in my improvised shelter, but it was of little avail. I was wet through and chilled to the bone. Yet I must have dozed off, for suddenly I became aware of rain falling. Unnoticed, the skies had clouded over and now the elements were completing our discomfiture. Ours was hardly an enviable situation; the swirling river behind, the enemy in front, the elements taking toll of what little strength remained. I attempted ineffectively to cover myself and the gun with my ground-sheet. Then I tried walking up and down to maintain circulation and prayed for the morning, which would surely end our sufferings one way or another. At last the rain cleared and there were signs of the approaching day in the eastern sky.

These were tense moments, but frankly I regarded the greatest dangers as those now in our rear. Fear had given way before the icy cold grip that now held me. In a short while it was daylight, and we were all alert and moving. The whole company lined up in sections with good spaces between. I told Smith, my Number Two and a new man, to stick to me like glue, and this indeed he did all through the subsequent action, as will be seen. The riverbed was now showing up clearly around us, while ahead we could see another stream. The horizon gradually widened as the last shadows of night receded. We began to fidget and fear that the enemy would spot us. But still nothing happened. Never surely had zero hour seemed so long in coming.

At last whistle blasts from our right signalled the advance and our officers waved us forward. Our guns opened out; an irregular line of white puffs began to spurt up some way ahead. We looked for the real barrage as we rushed forward, but it soon became clear that the ludicrous line of bursts was all the help we were likely to get. They were light calibre shells, falling at such wide intervals that a whole regiment could have passed between. They had nuisance value — to us not the enemy — and we cursed those gunners for their ineffectiveness.

We seemed to have lined up too far back and had to move quickly to catch up. The stream in front was wide but did not come above the knee at the deepest point. Whether it was because of the sudden movement after hours of inaction in the cold, I do not know, but I felt myself staggering and gasping under the weight of the gun. Captain Stirling, rushing forward and shouting encouragement to his company, saw my weakness and found the time in all that turmoil to call me by name, shouting not unkindly, 'Come on, we shall soon be there now'. This put heart into me. Little did I know that this was the last time I should hear his voice. In looking back I never recollect the captain talking to me personally except on the two occasions during those big battles of Asiago and the Piave, and cannot to this day account for his personal interest, for I was a shy retiring youngster never wishing to push myself forward. The captain's solicitude on those fearful occasions was the greatest honour I have received in all my life.

There was now a low bank ahead and some Austrians, presumably an advance post, came forward to give themselves up. This was our first sight of the enemy but still the expected storm of fire had not fallen upon us. I was amazed at the ease of our progress. The riverbank was reached. Then there arose a cry of dismay for, just beyond, a heavy belt of barbed wire rose up absolutely untouched by our artillery. Again we cursed those gunners.

Right ahead the wire receded into a bay, at the point of which there was a narrow opening left for the passage of Austrian patrols. There were probably other openings of this type, but this was the only one I saw. My new energy not having spent itself, I found myself moving towards this gap with the fixed idea of getting past the wire. Not an enemy shot had yet rung out ahead. Some fool — kindly fool, even in battle — shouted, 'It's certain death!' I hesitated, my bravery ran out and I fell back among the hesitating ranks. I got slightly bayoneted for my trouble, for one of the new hands, trailing his rifle like a pitchfork, ran the bayonet-point into the back of my right thigh, just deeply enough to make itself felt later in the day.

We bunched like sheep behind the barrier. Some made ineffective feints at the barbed strands with the special cutters affixed to their rifles, but nothing short of high explosive would have cleared a gap through that well-constructed barbed

wire fence many feet in depth. It was clear that the gaps would
have to be rushed. The enemy now took a hand. Slow-firing
machine guns began to traverse the wire. Something had to be
done. Men now rushed blindly into the gap, disappearing from
sight before my eyes like sand through an hourglass. Instead of
being first I was, with Smith, the last. I shouted to him through
the din and hurled myself at the gap. I soon saw that all had
not got through, and the rapid dissolving of the crowd around
was quickly explained. The wire-formed pocket was littered
with huddled khaki forms. One, who had fallen close upon the
wire, drooped limply, held up from the ground by the barbs
which gripped his uniform. Strangely — and fortunately for us
— the gap itself was perfectly clear. As I ran through the
narrow passageway the thick wire seemed to rise like beanstalks
on either side. I could see the bullets sparking waist-high
against the strands and pickets as the machine gun traversed
again. It was a miracle that we both escaped. For a brief
moment I caught a glimpse of a flat open ledge, on the far side
of which there ran a low embankment about a couple of
hundred yards away — the enemy position. The guns traversed
again. I flung myself to the ground and crawled towards a
shallow fold.

I saw no movement out in front, but over to the right, where
the wire veered sharply towards the enemy position, I had
noticed a number of men lying, obviously still alive and waiting
for something to happen. Among them not far away I saw
Sergeant Brittain, who, had he known it, was already in charge
of the company. It seemed certain death to stay where I was,
practically in front of the gap. Yet there was little chance of
better cover. Enemy machine guns and rifles were scouring the
surrounding ground, their bullets ricocheting in all directions. I
managed to crawl behind a low shrub, whose roots raised the

ground just a few inches. Smith, who had also got through uninjured, lay somewhere behind me, as I had learned from his shouts. Almost within reach to my right another soldier lay flat to the ground. A bullet entered his shoulder. As his body convulsed with pain, one of his legs bent upwards involuntarily and another bullet went through his ankle. He crawled away towards the wire groaning pitifully while I lay petrified across my gun, expecting a similar fate.

Like the drowning man I now had a thousand visions in what seemed hours but was probably not more than a minute or two. Time seemed to stand still. My position was clear: behind were the wires and behind them the river; in front were the enemy, secure in their defence line. Bullets continued to stream overhead. The day was young and we were sitting targets with little chance. It was not a very heroic position. I felt an overpowering weakness. Even if the opportunity came to make a sudden leap I had the gun to lift; and that — so my imagination worked — would make me a mark for every Austrian within sight. Shells, or trench mortar bombs, began to burst near the wires and I had visions of the barrage closing down upon us. Over to the left in the next bay a Lewis gun opened out with its deep rattle, only to stop abruptly. I was now in an agony of fear, seeing death in a dozen guises around me and not knowing what to do about it.

But already the situation was changing. Stretcher-bearers began to move about. The badly wounded figure of our bluff major began to drag itself over from the right towards the gap in the wire. Behind us the supporting troops were beginning to throw themselves through the gaps. The machine guns ahead had stopped firing. As I rose to my feet, the new arrivals were urging us forward and wisely taking the poor cover we were relinquishing. I stooped to lift my gun, and an age seemed to pass as I hoisted it laboriously to my shoulder. That is how things happen on a battlefield. It was as though an overwhelming pressure had suddenly been removed and we were reacting like automatons. What had been all stillness up to a moment before was now all movement. One was aware of only some of the things that were taking place. One thing however was certain: the whole line was again flowing towards the enemy positions.

The moving line was now agog with excitement, cheering as it swept across the open ground. On all sides men were rising from the earth, but there were some who would never rise again. Stretcher-bearers were already hard at work. I realised at once that safety depended upon our reaching the embankment ahead with the least possible delay. I called to Smith, who was close at hand, and we rushed forward shouting with the rest. We passed many recumbent figures, some writhing in agony. So great was the enthusiasm engendered by our release from inaction that even the wounded joined in. I saw one burly member of the company rise to a sitting position, though both his legs were soaked red with blood, and shout madly 'Forward the Eleventh!' From the left the enemy continued to pour a raking fire into our flank, but ahead the gunners had abandoned hope and were coming out to meet us, their arms waving above their heads. As they came through the advancing ranks, I saw a young soldier at my elbow lowering his bayonet with a shout of hatred and unmistakeable intention. I spurted, grasped his right arm as I passed, and just managed to deflect the point harmlessly aside. I shouted, 'He's a prisoner, you blasted fool! Save that for the others in front.'

We reached the embankment, which was about fifteen feet high and should have been a splendid defence line. It felt safer there against the slope. We spread along to the left and gradually the section collected together again. We had all become mixed up in the attack. Our luck had held, as the team only had one member wounded, although pretty badly according to accounts. Captain Stirling had been killed, as well as his second-in-command Lieutenant Hewitt, an old Guards officer, who had only rejoined us from brigade school for this last stunt. The only other officer with us had been badly wounded. The company had been shattered. We heard also that the battalion staff had been cut up, our colonel killed, the major severely wounded (as I had seen), and that among the officers only the padre, who had come over with us, remained unscathed.

It now devolved upon our few remaining NCOs to decide what should be done next, for none of us knew the actual plans. This was the first objective, but the situation was still a bit unusual since we had not yet actually occupied the position, as the trench was at the top of the embankment and we were collected along the foot. From the cover of the slope I looked back over the captured ground to where many bodies fringed the wires. Stretcher-bearers were running from case to case, with bullets still flying overhead. Just in front of the wires I could see the more regular formation of the supporting troops, and such was the clearness of the situation that I marvelled that the enemy had let a single one of us get through. The *Official History* points out that one of the weaknesses of this position was that the enemy was unable to direct his machine gun fire inside seventy yards from the embankment. That would have been sufficient at the point which we attacked, for the wire was further away than that, and in any case riflemen should have been able to keep us back. The Austrian seems to have been so confident of the security of his line that he had not taken all possible steps to make it properly defensible.

Enemy fire was still pouring in from the left and it was only the protecting bank before us that enabled us to form up and take a breather. As it was now known that this was the 'B' Company objective, the question was should we stay there according to plan or should we go forward with the next advance. In view of the changed position our corporal decided on going forward.

The troops on our right were preparing to advance again as soon as the so-called barrage lifted. It occurred to me that it would be a good idea to put up covering fire from the top of the embankment as the line moved forward. Lance-Corporal Westgarth raising no objection, I climbed the slope and got the gun into action. I could not see far beyond the embankment, since we were on the edge of an orchard and the trees came right up to the line at that point. I began to fire short bursts down into the orchard and was soon joined by others, who helped to put up a regular barrage, while the troops on the right moved forward again. This chance to do something materially assisted in raising my spirits. As I slipped back down the slope to replace my empty magazine and prepare to move forward my eye lit upon a truly fearful sight. The gunner who had been firing a few paces to my right had been hit in the head by a bullet that must certainly have come in enfilade from the left and therefore missed me by inches. He had slipped back head foremost down the slope. I recognised him as a member of one of the 'A' Company teams, whom I knew well by sight. The dark mass of his brain lay exposed, pulsing with his life's blood, and his eyes still seemed to hold a look of understanding. But he was beyond all human aid. Horrified, even among so much horror, I gathered my gun in my arms, climbed the bank again, scuttled over the skyline and sighed with relief as I slipped to the ground on the far side. There I waited while the rest of the section caught up. I had had a glimpse along the enemy trench as I crossed over. It was built into the top of the embankment, with good fire positions and shelters, and should have been impregnable. Now it was deserted, except for the dead bodies of those caught in the preliminary bombardment, which must have been much more serious than the fantastically light barrage which was supposed to be aiding us that morning.

We went forward among the trees. Over to the left heavy shells were falling, presumably from our own guns, to protect the open flank. Once or twice we found ourselves veering into this barrage and had to turn hastily rightwards. The light barrage had already gone ahead. A little way back we entered the close support positions — a machine gun emplacement. Two of the Austrian gunners, who lay dead in the trench, had been hit by a shell while preparing a meal. We removed the provisions with alacrity — a chunk of black bread fell to my share — while the less heavily burdened members scrounged for revolvers. Although here and there the weight of the recent bombardment had left its mark, the surrounding fields and orchards retained a rural charm, and we were already feeling very different in this open country warfare, which to us was a completely new experience. Despite our doubts as to where we ought to be, a new carefree attitude was taking control. We were no longer the frightened troops nailed to the earth by a storm of steel in many different forms. We were advancing into enemy-held territory, victors at last, after all those months and years of fear and stultification. Death was still about, perhaps only just round the corner, but the dice were no longer weighted against each one of us. It felt good to be alive on that sunny autumn morning on the Plains of Lombardy.

The advance had now become disorganised — if it had ever been otherwise. Occasionally we got glimpses of men moving among the trees away to our right. It was already evident that few of our own company had elected to leave the first objective; for besides the Lewis gun section there were only three or four riflemen with us, including one of the company runners. The expected opposition failed to materialise, the birds seemed to have flown. The orchard was well behind us. We were following a path alongside a small copse, when we turned a corner and ran bang into an enemy post. There were nine of us all told and by the normal laws of the game our over-confidence should have brought down a severe punishment on our heads. But no sooner did we appear than there issued from the strong point, about fifty yards ahead, a regular crowd of Austrians. There must have been thirty at least. Without waiting for the slightest menace on our part they came forward in a body with their arms stretched above their heads. It was such a funny sight that I could hardly refrain from laughing, but prudence bade us prepare for trouble and look for traps. However it soon became clear, from the expressions on their faces, that these men wanted to be well out of the war, and having assured ourselves that they were all unarmed we faced the knotty problem of how to dispose of them. One or two had shrapnel wounds and one was so badly hit that they had placed him on a stretcher. As one of our riflemen had a slight wound, it was decided that he should escort the prisoners back. The last we saw of him he was trailing behind with his bayonet held low and the crowd of Austrians streaming before him like a flock of sheep.

After this short delay we pushed forward quickly and at the edge of an extensive ploughed field came up with an officer and an NCO of another company, who were collecting stragglers before advancing across to the far hedge, which seemed a likely hide-out for the defence. We strung out in open order and continued our progress, expecting at any moment to hear the rattle of a machine gun ahead, but still nothing untoward happened. Coming in from the right — it was a characteristic of our flank position that everything came from the right that morning — we saw an officer approaching who, as he came nearer, we recognised as the battalion's VC; he had been wounded in the hand and was going back to the rear to have it dressed. We waved and wished him the best of luck, not without the usual streak of jealousy for his good fortune. Later I heard that he had been killed crossing one of the pontoons, which was receiving attention from the Austrian artillery. Such is the futility of military glory. A brave man dies by a chance shell as easily as a coward. Neither bravery nor cowardice are keys to survival in the days of high explosive.

We caught up with the diminutive barrage and tacked ourselves on to the left flank of the Durham Light Infantry, who were still going forward, although for the time being the barrage had halted. There were no more than a handful of Northumberlands there, perhaps twenty in all, although there may have been others mixed up with the Durhams. The barrage had stopped at the nearer edge of a large field. Nearby an officer, watch in hand, told us that this would lift shortly and then we should continue our advance. We lay in a shallow ditch, which afforded some cover from our own shells falling in the main a few yards ahead, although now and again one fell short behind us; not very dangerously but sufficiently nerve-racking to make one want to get on with the business. One could be within a couple of yards of one of those bursts without being hurt, and it was incredibly foolish to use such a barrage for protection. It may have had some use however in regulating the advance, for without it we should not have known where the front wave was supposed to be.

In the field in front there were a few trees in rows to break the horizon, while the ground rose just enough to obscure the opposite hedges. Not very far beyond there was an Austrian heavy battery firing from gun-pits, for we could see the smoke rising up after each discharge and hear the shells thundering away overhead to spread destruction in our rear. The Austrian artillerymen could not have been aware that they had no infantry between them and the advancing enemy, otherwise they would not have continued firing steadily and unconcernedly as they did. Presumably their field telephone had been dislocated.

At length the barrage took another jump forward. We followed at a steady pace, a few steps bringing us up the gently rising ground, whence the gun-pits could be clearly seen. Shouting to Smith, I dashed ahead of the advancing line, positioned my gun along the ground and fired a few bursts towards the battery, which immediately ceased firing. The mark was small, but I could just see the gunners' heads as they passed to and fro. My subsequent route did not take me into the gun-pits, but I heard from one of our men that one of the Austrians was wounded in the shoulder! They were all pleased enough to be taken prisoner.

The advance continued without opposition. We kept running into our barrage, such as it was, and not without danger, for a man near me got a piece of shrapnel in his body. Enemy machine guns were now working in front and over to the right, but the bullets flew high and I saw no one fall. Such incidents were too minor to diminish our confidence.

We reached another hedge, where the barrage had again come to a halt. At the further side of the next field we could see farm buildings and a line of trees. Bullets whistled overhead. It looked like resistance at last. The infantry lined up ready to go forward again, while a Stokes mortar gun was brought up to shell the farmhouse. It was positioned in the ditch alongside our section and we watched the movements with interest. Almost immediately an enemy transport wagon drove into the field towards the farmhouse. Too late the driver realised his mistake and tried to turn back. It looked for the moment as though he was bringing a gun into position to fire directly at us. In our excited state we were not very perceptive and a score of rifles cracked simultaneously. The driver and horses fell, and the wagon was seen in all its pathetic harmlessness.

Our presence having thus been disclosed, it was decided to advance at once to the last objective without waiting for the barrage to lift. The trench mortar gun commenced shelling the farm, and after some argument the Lewis gun team decided to stay and support them. The decision was not mine, although I did not in the least mind staying in the rear of our own shells. Short of direct instructions we had some excuse for dallying, but not much. The Stokes' canisters smashed into the farm as the line went steadily across the field against a counter flow of machine gun bullets, which streamed overhead. The troops soon disappeared from sight, the officer gave orders to cease fire, and the battery packed up straight away and were led off to our right, leaving us alone.

Now we should certainly have resumed our advance but we didn't. A stream of prisoners came running unaccompanied down the field. Some were wounded. We searched them for arms and made them turn out their pockets, taking from their pocket-wallets a number of bank notes of the type specially printed by the Austrians for the occupied territories. They were clean from the mint and some were for such low values as five and ten *centissimi*. We knew these were only of interest as souvenirs and we handed back the bulk to their owners, together with any purely personal objects. These Austrians were in a shocking state of nerves, wincing every time one of the troublesome Italian shells burst nearby. We motioned them to continue their way back over on their own, and this they did with gratitude and alacrity.

The lance-corporal was becoming fidgety, naturally enough. What ought we to do? Our front wave had disappeared and only the sound of enemy machine guns indicated any movement in that direction. Behind, all was still; we had no idea where the supports were, if any. On our left, to, all was quiet. It was from that direction that we were expecting the Italians to sweep in, but still there was no movement. We were now an isolated group without contact in any direction, and again wished we had stayed back at the first objective with the remnants of the company. We decided to wait and put our arms in order. My leg was stiffening and, although on examination there was little to show, I limped throughout the rest of the day. The shelling lifted at last and then an enemy machine gun began to play across the field, providing a further excuse for lying low.

At long last an officer came hurrying down the field accompanied by an orderly. His mission was to find out what was happening in the rear, but we could not enlighten him. He told us that the line had halted at the final objective only a couple of hundred yards or so ahead, and ordered us to join up with them. It was a breathless scamper across the field under a spray of machine gun bullets, which were certainly firing high, for no one was hit. We were fortunate in this, though one is not to know at the time that the danger is less than it appears.

We gained the cover of a slight depression down the left-hand side of the field and worked along to a roadway at the end. That road — a typical tree-lined second-class highway — was now the front line, its further ditch being occupied by a thin row of khaki-clad figures. We found a mixed collection of our own battalion on the left flank of the line, which now extended some sixty or seventy yards to a crossroads on our left, where the last post of the whole Allied line rested. The Italians had still not arrived and we were beginning to wonder what had happened to them. An NCO ordered the gun section to a spot in the line where it was thin, and we took stock of our new position.

Over to the right I could see the men of the Durhams lining the ditch, which trailed out of sight in a vista of trees. Now and again a figure, officer or NCO, stretcher-bearer or runner, detached itself from the line and moved quickly along the road, but it obviously paid to keep well into the ditch since enemy machine guns continued to rattle out in front. Straight ahead there were bare fields but one could not see very far. We were told that scouting parties had been forward without contacting the enemy and that there was a village not far away, which, it was thought, could have been occupied without difficulty. But we were now at the day's objective and no further orders had been issued. In fact, for all the definite information we had about the progress of the battle, the front wave could have been lost in the void. That is certainly how we felt.

I thought of food now and was keenly upset when I discovered that, in the recent scurry, I had lost the piece of black bread captured from the enemy. Our conversation turned to the events of the morning, and we realised even more clearly than hitherto how badly we had been cut up and how many of the old hands had been killed or severely wounded. Many of the youngsters of the last draft had also gone, in their very first smell of action, but we were unanimous in agreeing that they had behaved wonderfully. The loss of all our officers and the majority of our NCOs was much regretted. Only a handful of 'B' Company were in this advanced position, although a few others straggled in later.

Some of the men had slight wounds and were eager to get back for attention as soon as opportunity should arise. But there was one very seriously wounded, a prisoner whose head was swathed in blood-stained bandages. He was dazed and, from the look in his eyes, it seemed that his mind was wandering. He looked from one to another of us and cried plaintively, 'Wasser, Wasser'. No one offered the poor devil any. We all knew how precious our small store might become during the operations. I had half a bottle still and inwardly wished to offer some, but was actually afraid of playing Philip Sidney in front of my companions. I refused him too, and ever since have wished I had not. I can still see those eyes, staring pitifully. He was taken back shortly afterwards with our wounded, and though I hardly think he could have survived, miracles did sometimes happen and I hope so much that he did.

A sergeant came along with orders for advance posts to be put out in front. On direct instructions I crawled forward with the gun, accompanied by Smith, until they shouted from the road for us to stop. This new position was a poor one; we could see very little in front. Whether we were under observation I cannot tell, but a machine gun began suspiciously to play across the field, forcing us to flatten ourselves to the ground. We could do no good there and were glad when all the advanced posts were called back. Our position in the line was weak enough. Short of ammunition and out of touch with our supports — if there were any — we had little power to meet a counterattack.

The long day was now drawing to a close. The sun, which had shone down brightly upon us since the early morning, was sinking to our left, and bluish shadows were gathering at the foot of the trees. Out in front each moving branch seemed to indicate the presence of an enemy, whose distant machine guns continued to play across the road. Over to our left, one much closer at hand began to rap out a baleful tattoo. There, too, from the open flank enemy lights began to punctuate the gathering gloom.

I was now ordered to reinforce the flank at the crossroads where our line ended. There we held a little bridge crossing a narrow stream, which was the target of the Austrian machine gun. On the way along we met two fully-equipped Austrians under escort. They had been returning from leave to join their unit in the line when they just walked into our outposts. Their surprise can be imagined, and certainly this unusual incident was very reassuring to us, for it showed that, far from staging the routine counterattack at the moment of danger, the enemy did not even know where his own positions were.

We had hardly carried out our new order and cast our eyes upon the bridge when a runner literally leapt from nowhere and issued the welcome command that all members of 'B' Company should make their way back to the support line. There were no more than a dozen of us in all. The runner, acting as guide, set off but it was now dark and not easy to pick one's way across strange ground. There was the ever-present danger of running off our territory into an enemy post on the left flank. After wandering about in the dark for some time we suddenly saw a light glimmering from the ground ahead of us. The shadowy form of a dismantled gun revealed one of the captured gun emplacements. The light came from a dug-out opening, which we approached, hoping to obtain definite information as to our whereabouts. An indescribably weird sight met my gaze through the dugout door. It was a large chamber, illuminated by a number of candles stuck about in various positions, some spluttering to their dying glint while others, more recently lit, shone out steadily. The whole dugout was filled with a glimmering blueness that contrasted queerly with the outside blackness. It was crammed full of Austrians in every possible posture — sitting, kneeling, reclining — each swathed in bandages whose whiteness seemed to collect the reflected candle-light. It is difficult to convey the absolute unreality of that assembly of enemy wounded, gathered there in preference to braving the hazards of bombardment in the rear areas of the battlefield.

They continued to converse in gutteral tones and took no notice of our intrusion. We were tired and it seemed no business of ours. Shortly afterwards we reached our support line and were welcomed back to the fold. Yet there could have been serious consequences to follow, for who could really be confident that those Austrians were incapable of offensive action? Nothing shows more clearly the haphazard nature of the battle situation at the end of that first day of the advance.

HISTORICAL NOTE: THE FINAL BATTLE

29 October 1918 is recognised by Austrian historians as the decisive day of the final battle on the Italian front, the main event being the defeat by the British of the XVI Corps of the Isonzo Army on the Monticano. Increasing difficulties inside the Habsburg dominions strengthened Austria-Hungary's decision that evening that Venetia should be evacuated.

So far as the remainder of the front was concerned the only considerable advance on 29 October was made by the Italian Eighth Army across the Montello sector of the Piave front, thus considerably broadening the area of pressure on the enemy. These troops had drawn level with the main line of advance by nightfall, and in the centre had even been able to push forward a light column of lancers and Bersaglieri cyclists to seize Vittorio Veneto, a key village about ten miles from the Piave, from which the whole battle takes its name. On the British right the Italian XI Corps, part of Lord Cavan's command, were assigned limited objectives on the flank, which was now being dragged back because no crossing of the lower Piave had yet been made by the Italian Third Army, which occupied all the remainder of the Allied line down to the sea.

On 30 October both the 23rd and 7th British Divisions continued to advance. The Corps' mounted troops reached the outskirts of Sarcile, on the Livenza, soon after midday, but after an initial success was forced to withdraw before an enemy counterattack and to await the arrival of the infantry. Resistance was encountered as they approached the river and a private of the Royal Welch Fusiliers was hit, earning the doubtful honour of being the last man of the 7th Division to be killed in the 1914-1918 War. On the left of Lord Cavan's troops the Italians were now pressing forward steadily. Their Eighth and Twelfth Armies — the latter including the French 23rd Division — were following the retreating Austrians into the mountains, but to their left the Italian Fourth Army were still being held on the Monte Grappa front.

On the following day the Livenza was crossed and the 23rd Division fired its last shots in the war. The entire Allied line from Monte Grappa to the sea was now moving forward towards the Tagliamento, which was crossed on 4 November, the British troops in this last drive (from the 7th Division) being the 1st Royal Welch Fusiliers, the Royal Warwickshires and the 2nd Border Regiment. On their right was the American 332nd Regiment, which had joined the battle but was destined, owing to the sudden ending of the war, to see little fighting. This is certainly not the impression one gets from reading Ernest Hemingway's colourful and celebrated, but highly misleading, novel *A Farewell to Arms*.

In the mountains far away to the west, on the night of 30 October, the Austrians had begun withdrawing from their Asiago positions, with the intention of holding their prepared *Winterstellung* positions a little way to the rear. During the following day fires amidst the hills and desultory shelling indicated that something important was afoot. British patrols went forward to maintain contact with the enemy and on 1 November the French 24th and the British 48th Divisions (which had been left up in the mountains for this purpose) launched a heavy attack. After a brave initial resistance the Austrian defences were pierced at vital points. It was too late for the Austrians to save the situation. The battle became a pursuit, the British troops pressing deeply into the mountains, and by 2 November the Austrian frontier had been crossed. During this spectacular breakthrough the 48th Division, for the loss of one officer and 25 men killed, 129 wounded and 7 missing, captured over twenty thousand prisoners and a tremendous number of guns. Such statistics provide a sure measure of the Austrian morale.

An armistice with Austria was signed on 3 November, to come into operation at 3pm the next day. Already on 30 October, as a result of a successful drive by British troops in Mesopotamia and of General Allenby's great victories in Palestine and Syria, an armistice had been signed with the Turks. The Hungarians had split away from the Austro-Hungarian Empire, which was in rapid dissolution. Finally at 5 am on 11 November, in a train in the Forest of Compiegne, an armistice was signed between the Allies and Germany, and an unearthly silence fell all along the battle line, from the Swiss frontier to the Dutch border.

10: THE VICTORY OF VITTORIO VENETO

The somewhat inadequate support trench was masked in front by a hedge, which had of course been behind the Austrian defence position. Thus our outlook was obscured, although from our gun post we could at least see down the field in front. In this trench line the remnants of 'A' and 'B' Companies were now gathered. Over to our right a much-depleted battalion headquarters were occupying a shattered farmhouse and outbuildings. The night was cold, as was to be expected at that time of year. Enemy machine guns chattered sporadically out in front, while bursts of rifle fire from our own front line indicated that they were far from confident about the enemy's intentions. Occasionally a hostile battery came into action, dropping shells uncomfortably close, while shrapnel bursts spattered the skies away ahead of us. Enemy lights rose and fell all along the horizon, sweeping in close upon our left and far behind, giving an impression of encirclement that was far from reassuring.

I huddled on the trench bottom, a narrow roughly-made ditch, and, dazed with fatigue, dozed throughout the night, depending upon my closely wrapped ground-sheet to keep in what little warmth there was. I had a half-waking consciousness of sentries being changed but, by some stroke of fortune, was not bothered until just before dawn. I was then so chilled that it was with difficulty that I clambered on to the parapet, where I staggered up and down in a half-conscious state for some minutes before my full senses returned. The whine of bullets and the crash of a shell directed towards the adjacent buildings — an obvious target for the Austrian gunners — caused me to realise my exposed position and to stumble back into the trench.

With the first signs of dawn in the skies, orders to stand to passed along the trench, which was soon bursting with life. Bayonets began to glint in the morning rays as the battlefield re-emerged from obscurity. Birds twittered in neighbouring hedgerows, untouched by battle, and a cool breeze rustled autumn leaves, in startling contrast to my previous war experience. With the first bright gleams of the sun the last enemy light had faded, and also the likelihood of counterattack, for which we had fearfully watched. More shells screamed over. Rifle fire out in front heralded the new day.

Almost immediately came heartening news. A runner with orders for battalion headquarters told us that the Italian army which had failed to cross on our north flank was now coming up behind us, across the Island of Papadopoli (where we had crossed yesterday), to launch their own attack from this very position in a turning movement across our flank to clear the territory still held by the enemy. Tension relaxed. We cheered the news. The people behind were doing things after all, and yesterday's sacrifices were not to be in vain. Previous disappointing experiences were not to be repeated on this occasion. For we who had so far survived, these were thrilling moments.

We withdrew from the line, the Lewis gun team being fortunate to find a ready-made firepit only a few yards back, so positioned that we should be out of the way and yet able to watch the forthcoming manoeuvre.

Shortly the head of the Italian column arrived and was received with great enthusiasm. They were indeed fortunate to launch an attack with such encouragement. The newcomers looked smart and well-armed, and took the situation as a matter of course, apparently not fully aware of their good fortune at having missed the rushing waters of yesterday. We had no doubt that they meant business. Heavily burdened with brand-new equipment, much of which they dumped in the field nearby, they took up positions along the hedge that bordered the left hand side of the field, stretching away to the rear. A barrage was expected, and suddenly it fell around us, a swishing wall of light shells, making us seek the trench bottom. As usual it started too far back, causing the assembled attackers to draw back in some confusion. Fortunately the guns were again firing those comparatively innocuous shells of the day before, although now there were more of them, and the setback was therefore merely momentary. The silly barrage quickly moved beyond the hedge and the Italians melted from sight. Machine guns began to rattle and rifles to crack, as streams of supports flowed after the first line. The movement continued intermittently throughout the morning: infantry in large numbers, machine-gun groups, mule-drawn mountain batteries, Red Cross units. Never had I been in a position to see such a host pouring on to a battlefield. Within a few minutes of the start, counter-streams had begun to flow back; many wounded limping or stretcher-borne, but above all Austrians — hundreds of them — indicating that there had been large concentrations near at hand, numerous enough to have swamped us had they had any enterprise. What a missed opportunity! In the meantime our 10th Battalion, which had been guarding the flank, filed through to our own front where, we heard, the line was again moving forward. The noise of battle gradually receded and it was evident that the enemy were falling back rapidly.

It was time to reorganise ourselves, for that is what we were there for now, but our first care was to look after our own comfort. The firepit seemed as suitable a shelter as we were likely to find in the vicinity, especially as we could now supplement our defences against the cold and damp with blankets and waterproof bivouac sections from the heaps dumped by the Italians before their attack. Long range guns occasionally dropped a heavy shell near the farmhouse. Enemy aircraft flew over to attack the bridges. There were reports of heavy casualties as the bombs crashed down on to the river crossings, and this counterblast was sufficiently successful to prevent our supporting artillery and transport from moving forward.

'B' Company, now all assembled, had been reduced to less than half. Apart from the leaders, already mentioned, the killed included the cocky little private, whom I had witnessed steadying the company during our last helter-skelter withdrawal from the Passchendaele trenches the previous autumn. This truculent, boastful, not very popular fellow had but a few weeks previously told the whole billet what he would do to the Austrians during our next battle, swearing that he would win the Victoria Cross or die in the attempt. Now he had kept his word, and for all that can ever be known, possibly on both counts, for he was of the rare type that knew not fear.

The reorganised battalion was now placed under the command of a major from the Durhams. The remnants of 'A' and 'B' Companies were reformed into one company, our particular contribution amounting to eight sections, for which we had only seven NCOs available, including Sergeants Brittain and Goffee. Westgarth was switched to take charge of one of the rifle sections, while I was surprised and proud to receive charge of the only Lewis gun section, without change

233

of rank. I was truly sorry, however, to lose Smith, who had behaved so splendidly as Number Two, but his place as guardian of the spare parts was taken by Virtue, who had been among those transferred from the Army Service Corps before we left France and who was to behave just as reliably. For myself, I was glad that this arrangement enabled me to retain hold of the gun, for I had learned yesterday that in open country warfare the NCO in command was liable to become little more than a supernumerary.

We were now actually in reserve and our second night in the position passed off without incident. We had made our detached trench very cosy with the Italian blankets, while our slight isolation had left us out of the sentry rota, which of course now needed to be less highly organised. Consequently we awoke in better condition than we had experienced for some time, but very hungry. Fortunately our indefatigable Company Quartermaster Fail had managed to get some supplies through: there were biscuits and cheese for breakfast. We had welcomed the arrival of the carrying party with enthusiasm, for they had accomplished a difficult task.

Orders now came for us to move forward again. The brigade was being held up on the Monticano stream and it was to be our mission to clear the way. Our chief chagrin in the circumstance was in being forced to discard our recently acquired Italian treasure trove.

We now had the novel experience of marching forward into country just evacuated by the enemy. Apart from a few desultory shell-bursts there was little to show that we were crossing a battlefield. Trees and hedges, even buildings, appeared to be intact, though on closer inspection the latter often disclosed gaping holes or a spatter of rifle bullets in the outer walls. We kept to the roads, eventually reaching a row of low buildings, where a halt was called. Here there were a few Italian civilians, much elated by the march of events, and some Austrians, a few of whom could speak English, who could hardly have cared less. They included a number of Poles and Czechs, whose patriotism for the dwindling Austro-Hungarian Empire was at low ebb. Our halt proved to be well timed, for we were able to have a snack, even to wash. One of the houses had been an inn, and was still not completely denuded of vino. Naturally it had become a collecting point for all and sundry, mainly NCOs and runners from the various units on their way somewhere. There was much discussion of what was happening up in front and it was generally held that the enemy were in full retreat.

Soon after moving off again we were entering the battle zone and the appearance of things changed as if by magic — black magic. Our route lay through a considerable village, which was being pasted with heavy shells. We went through at the double in artillery formation. Walls were tumbling all around, as shells crashed into the brickwork. Smoke flowed out of the ruins across the ploughed-up roadway and for a brief while we imagined ourselves back on the Western Front. The enemy, who were doing their utmost to stop the onflow of supporting troops, were undoubtedly making a desperate stand at this point.

We were glad to leave behind the built-up area, but signs of bloodshed increased with every step. The tree-lined road, running straight as a die, was being subjected to a heavy barrage of both high explosive and shrapnel and, as I have said before, the Austrians were good with their artillery. The route, in the way of Italian highways, formed a sort of causeway above the level of the bordering countryside, and our need for speed rendered it impossible to tackle the alternative obstacles of the fields with their irrigation ditches.

At this point the company was rallied by CQMS Fail who, transcending his normal function of supplies officer, had insisted upon coming up with us. We trickled forward on the right-hand edge of the road, while a counter-stream of wounded and prisoners passed rearwards on our left. Some of the wounded looked pretty bad, with blood-soaked bandages and ashen faces. A shell had just struck the road, catching members of this counter-stream, whose mangled bodies lay mashed upon the stones. Some of the walking-wounded belonging to another brigade eyed us fiercely. 'So you've come at last,' they shouted with utter contempt. 'Yes, at first as well,' we shouted back, stung even deeper by the injustice of their imputation. Despite the danger I felt like stopping and arguing it out with them!

We were now practically in front of the enemy barrage. The Monticano lay right across our path. Although not more than about twenty yards across at this point, the stream formed a pretty formidable obstacle. It flowed between high banks, whose sides would not have been easily scalable in face of determined fire. On the left our 10th Battalion had been held up, while the attacking forces to the right had already crossed. The Austrian rear-guard in front were in a position to harass this advancing flank, which probably accounted for the large flow of wounded. It was our task to go in at the hinge and clear the front ahead of the 10th Battalion.

We forded the stream at a suitable spot at the end of the road. We were now beyond the range of our own field guns and had to do without artillery support, but there was nothing falling near from the opposite direction. As we went up the steep opposite bank we expected to be welcomed by a fusillade from the rim above us, but all remained quiet. The enemy had decided that nothing more could be done and had withdrawn from the bank, which was eaten into by a row of funk-holes littered with spent cartridges. One contained a steel helmet; another a few yards away was still occupied by its defender, who had dropped limply forward with a bullet through his brain.

We turned away from the stream looking expectantly to the far hedges. These we reached, apprehensively and wonderingly without further incident. Our field of view was never extensive, for in this country all the fields were fringed with trees. Our difficulty now was to decide the proper direction for our advance. Beyond the hedge a sergeant, wishing to show initiative, directed us along a cart track leading rightwards. I was beginning to fan out my section into the long grass on the left of the track when a burst of machine-gun fire mowed through it, and we instantly found cover. The presence of the enemy having been discovered in this silly haphazard way, we were ordered to withdraw, while the officers, without plans and confused among themselves, began to issue contradictory orders, until we were even further mixed up. Fortunately the battalion commander now arrived on the scene and gave orders for a further withdrawal while he took stock of the position. No doubt our unexpectedly easy crossing of the stream had put everything out of balance.

A leftwards skirmishing movement into country where the retreating Austrians were known to be holding a number of farmhouses was now decided upon. But our extemporised company seemed quite incapable of grappling with this new type of warfare. The commanding officer, losing his temper — justifiably in the circumstances — threatened to send the officers back and to take direct control himself. The sections were now got into open formation, a whistle blew and we again moved forward. We were unable to see far towards our flanks but the movement of troops in parallel could be sensed beyond the hedges. Our orderly progress soon received a check. On the far side of the field we came to a tree barrier bordering a fast flowing irrigation channel. It was only a few feet wide, but the banks were steep and the thick hedge prevented us, burdened as we were, from crossing with a flying leap. The section on our right began to file across on a lock gate, which made a good bridge, but this movement seemed absurd to me with the enemy probably watching our every action. To set a good example I decided to lead my section through the stream just ahead. The water was limpid and the bottom seemed near enough. Yet no one could have been more surprised than I when I felt the cold water running above my waist and myself floundering against a strong current, while doing all I could to keep the gun from being immersed. I was ignominiously manhandled out of the stream by the two men behind me, and felt little of a hero when I followed the others across the lock gate.

We now found ourselves in the narrow end of a field that fanned out widely at the far side, and the redeployed line had advanced about a third of the way when a machine gun began to traverse across our front. No one was hit as far as I could see, but by all the rules we should have been decimated. At point-blank range the shooting was hopeless, but the bullets were ricocheting sufficiently close to keep our heads down. I crawled sideways like a crab to the hedge on our right, dragging the gun after me. There I slithered into a ditch filled with water, while the enemy gun continued to play across the now deserted field. The troops on our right, whom I could see through the belt of saplings, were also held up. The traversing machine gun was now joined by a light mountain battery, which began firing point blank down the field. Its miniature shells burst disconcertingly about the hedge, more like large explosive bullets than actual shells. One exploded within a couple of yards without doing the least damage, though a direct hit would have made mess enough. Crash-screech-pop! Crash-screech-pop! The Austrians blazed away, too excited to take proper aim, for again I saw no casualties. We stood, or rather lay on the ground, so far without replying.

Then a sergeant shouted for a Lewis gun to fire in support, while the men worked down the hedge towards the enemy. I crawled out into the field, set up the gun on its bipod and began to fire short bursts towards the point where the smoke was rising. Then the gun jammed. I had what was known as a stoppage, one of the drawbacks of that otherwise excellent weapon. Feverishly I worked, while another gun took up the firing. With the loose parts spread on the grass about my chin, I could not help wondering what would happen at that juncture should a retirement be ordered. But it was at such moments that our innumerable practices out of the line came to be fully justified. One went to work automatically and methodically and the gun became complete again. I had just reassembled the bolt and snapped the butt back into position when the line rose to the attack. We swept down the field with a shout, but the Austrians did not wait. The other Lewis gunnner sprawled down ahead of me, with the apparent intention of firing through the advancing ranks. He thought he could see the enemy moving beyond the hedge. Such a risky manoeuvre was much against my own professional ideas. I kicked him in the ribs as I passed, substituting for a stream of bullets a flow of obscene language and possibly saving some of our men from being shot up from the rear.

When we reached the hedge the enemy had again cleared out, leaving a pile of cartridge cases where the gun had been positioned. With hedges and irrigation channels criss-crossing everywhere, this was admirable country for defence, but the enemy, who were about in force, were making a poor job of it. As far as I heard the whole battalion suffered only two casualties in all the skirmishing — a corporal killed and a private wounded, somewhere on our left flank.

We now crossed a ploughed field with a copse to our right and a fringe of high trees at the far end. Into these I fired a magazine, as much to confirm that the gun was again in working order, as to find any sort of target, and we continued our advance without hindrance. Sergeant Goffee now took the lead. We abandoned open order for the shelter of the hedges, a method we should have adopted from the first. Batches of the enemy now began to appear from all directions without arms, and practically the entire enemy rearguard gave themselves up without our having to fire another shot. It was an amazing situation. The battalion continued busily to collect the spoils, and we learned later that we had taken more prisoners than our own strength.

Some of us continued to move forward. Away ahead of us there stood a large house masked by trees. There was no movement in the vicinity as we drew cautiously towards the large wooden door, which was shut fast, though we could hear murmuring within. Two of our number took up a stout log that had been prepared for fuel, while the sergeant and the team stood round with revolver and bayonets pointed towards the door. We called upon the occupants to surrender and, as there was no response, the battering ram was driven into the woodwork. At the very first impact the door flew open, to disclose a remarkable sight. We were looking into a large kitchen packed with humanity — women, children, old men and a couple of Austrian soldiers. The latter looked frightened, as well they might, but we just sent them back to join the rest of the prisoners.

The peasants now surged around and mobbed us. They shook our hands, still encumbered with weapons, shouting 'Americani?' 'Americani?' 'No, Inglesi,' we replied, and they looked with astonishment. We were in grave danger of being embraced. 'Come on,' shouted the embarrassed sergeant 'let's get out of this!' At this very moment an idiot, who had worked his way round to the back of the house, threw a Mills bomb, probably at a shadow, and with the crash the civilians scuttled indoors in terror.

Our route continued along the track and across another field into an orchard. It was dusk and there was now only a small party of us so far forward. The further end of the orchard was bounded by an embankment, from which we must have been spotted before coming under the cover of the trees. A field battery just beyond began firing with open sights into the trees. The shells burst frighteningly above, but fortunately we were far enough forward to miss the shrapnel. Then the guns, having delivered their final hate, ceased fire, and we heard the hasty movement of horses and wheels as the battery limbered up and moved off into the night.

We were now wandering in the darkness out of contact with friend or foe. A runner, who happened to stumble across us, said that the battalion had been ordered to halt. Our lefthand company were occupying a building two or three hundred yards away and it seemed wise to join them there. When we arrived our colleagues were all comfortably bedded down inside. No one would have imagined that there was no force between us and the enemy. A small enemy patrol could have captured the lot.

I was shortly collared by a strange sergeant-major, who had recently had acquaintance with a rum bottle. He ordered me to remain on sentry outside with the gun. There were only three of us together now, including Virtue, who had only one spare magazine. We could not have arrested the most anaemic rush. In response to a request for more ammunition the unsteady warrant officer told me that there was none. Annoyed at being treated in this way, I pointed out that I belonged to another company. He blasphemed and threatened to have me arrested if I continued to argue. A rifleman was now added to our force and the four of us patrolled outside the house, while the rest slumbered. I continued to fume, annoyed more at the demonstration of incompetence than anything else. But we had our compensation, though we did not realise it at the time.

The night was cold and clear, the air above us literally sparkled. Sounds of tractors and other transport moving away along the roads came clearly through the night, while here and there a light shot up, usually some distance back, suggesting that the enemy were unsure of our positions. The skies were suffused with the red glow of burning materials, of enemy dumps alight, sure signs that a full retreat had now been ordered. It was a wonderful, unforgettable experience to be standing there, a foremost post of an advancing army with only the retiring enemy ahead. A conscious thrill of victory ran down my spine, for those sounds of mechanical withdrawal and those flaming skies meant more than a retreating army. A great cloud seemed to be lifting from my soul. I was no longer afraid.

After some time a relief came out of the house, which we immediately entered. It was packed with sleepers, but we managed to find vacant floor space and fell immediately into deep sleep. Half-awake some time later I had a hazy impression, as one does on such occasions, that someone was trying to find us for another spell. 'Not my company,' I decided, not altogether justly, and snored vigorously. Later there was even greater bustle. Outside I could hear the clanking of equipments. The 10th Battalion were going through: we were no longer in front, and all was well.

Early the next morning we went in search of 'B' Company, which we knew was somewhere to the right. On the way we entered a house in search of information and were surprised to find the kitchen crammed with appreciative country folk and a number of Tommies. We scrounged a breakfast of *polenta*, which one of the women was making in a large pot, paying with official Italian money, with which the people were highly delighted. They gave us large notes of Austrian currency as change. This was our first meal since the previous morning. After further wanderings and some misdirections, we at last found the company drawn up on the main road awaiting the order to march. They greeted us vigorously, having feared that we had been captured by the enemy. Everybody was in the best of spirits. A nearby signpost pointed to Conegliano, which happened to be marked on my diminutive map, and I was able to realise for the first time the extent of the brigade's three-day forward drive.

Italian cavalry, cyclists and motorised machine gun units began to stream through in fine array, pressing forward in pursuit of the retreating enemy. For this moment of mobility these particular arms had waited long, and now their hour had arrived. It was a moment of unbounded enthusiasm, of unselfish elation, for we knew we were all sharing in a great experience. Then came the good news that our artillery had got across the Piave.

That morning we hung about for some time, and for once we did not mind. We did not know then, of course, but we had seen the last of the fighting and the battle line was flowing steadily ahead. In the meantime rations and mail came up, further evidence of the indefatigable efforts of our CQMS, who had now resumed his proper functions. To most, the cigarette ration was the crowning blessing of the day.

Late in the afternoon orders came to move forward. As we passed through the villages all the people came out to line the route and cheer. Though the Austrians had not been hard taskmasters, the Italians were understandably not in good shape. Food and comforts had not been abundant behind the enemy lines. The houses, in the main untouched, wore an air of utter emptiness. In a field at one point a multitude of vehicles had been gathered, a nondescript collection of all sorts of contraptions on wheels, from wheelbarrow to farm cart, mostly dilapidated. What had been the intention of this assemblage? They had just been left derelict, not even destroyed. Perhaps it was just an instinctive veto on all possible mobility on the part of the Austrian authorities. Large batches of forlorn prisoners were continually flowing back past us.

In the evening the skies were again afire with burning dumps and lights were going up all over the place, some not very far away, suggesting that the retreat was ragged and our contact patchy. That night we billeted in a large house that had been fitted out as a telephone exchange. It was in a small place on the railway, whose name I did not note down. Some houses had been gutted. Near the station large dumps of enemy stores were still burning fiercely.

We spent the next day making ourselves ship-shape and exploring the neighbourhood for souvenirs. We were proud to receive, direct from the GOC, a message of congratulation to the battalion — 'Magnificent' — and our thoughts went back to the dead who had done so much to earn it. During the night Italian armoured cars thundered through the village, indicating that increasing pressure was being exerted on the Austrian rearguards.

On the morning of 1 November, the brigadier-general came to address the battalion. He told us how our dead commander, Lieutenant-Colonel St. Hill, and he had been personal friends for many years and had served together in the East. Hill, he told us with deep emotion, had been every inch a soldier, whose first thoughts had always been for his battalion. He had, he well knew, a reputation for strictness, but never had he hazarded a life without good cause. He had been proud of his battalion, and his battalion had very good reason to be proud of him. It did not fall to the lot of every battalion commander to lead his men personally into action, but often he (the brigadier) had had difficulty in restraining his friend from taking greater risks than his important position warranted. At this point the speaker broke down sobbing, and there could have been few dry eyes in the listening ranks. While the brigadier was speaking, I, for one, could not resist a strong feeling that we had often misjudged our dead leader, whose austere demeanour had hardly recommended him to the ranks, and I was sorry.

When we continued our march on 2 November, now far to the rear, the Austrians were expected to make a stand on the Tagliamento river. There were now fewer signs of conflict, but during the morning we came upon a spectacle that, in contrast to the placid countryside, heightened the normal horrors of war — the piled debris of an enemy artillery column which had been caught by our planes. Could it have been the battery that had tried to shoot us up in the orchard? Large holes had been blown into the roadway and alongside by a number of bombs and the whole detachment still lay there in utter confusion, heavy guns and loaded waggons overturned like so many nine-pins. Among them was the post cart with the Royal Hapsburg posthorn, the road round about being strewn with letters, many of them no doubt from beloved ones addressed to those who had since been killed. All were now being heedlessly trampled by passing traffic. Dark blood patches stained the side track, where the bodies of the unfortunate men and horses had been piled and the movable materials had been thrust aside to clear a way. In such a setting all this struck greater horror than the much more terrible carnage of a real battlefield. Yet these gunners had been used to directing their fire from comparative safety upon troops and others who had no means of personal retaliation. There was nothing heroic about this sort of thing. The machine was just working normally.

At the river crossing at Sarcile we crossed the improvised bridge and saw the holed church tower, from which enemy machine gunners had made their last stand. Already the town was agog with troops in Allied uniforms, including a high proportion of red-tabs, for several military headquarters were being established there.

Large batches of Austrian prisoners were continually passing under escort, as well as numbers of liberated Italian prisoners, who told us they had been held since Caporetto. This turn of events must have come as a great surprise, for they are not likely to have been given much war news by their captors. Our night's billet was a small cowshed in Porcia, a little place just this side of Pordenone. We were fortunate to find good supplies of clean straw, for being still in battle order, we were without blankets or top coats. Our bread ration had been drastically cut to aid the citizenry, who had been completely cleaned out of food, and in consequence our money was quite useless for supplementing our rations. But there was a ready market for Austrian revolvers scrounged during the battle, particularly with the Army Service Corps and other 'back area' troops.

On 3 November, which was a Sunday, detachments of the American regiment passed along the main road towards the line. They shouted with their usual arrogance that they had come to finish the war for us; we shouted back that they were a bit late, not realising even then how right we were. Rumours were passing around that Turkey had given in. During the afternoon the two old companies, combined as 'Z' Company, paraded for inspection by our new commander, a major, this time from the 10th Battalion.

On the following day we heard the wonderful news that the Austrians had been granted an armistice, though we were not yet clear whether an armistice was anything more than a temporary arrangement. This had come as a surprise, for though we well knew that the enemy had collapsed before us, the situation was so confused and impersonal, and past experience gave us no clue to the possibilities, that we found it difficult to believe it could all end just like this. Moreover, we knew enough about the great enemy way back in the rear to make it difficult to visualise his giving up as a consequence of Austria's failure. Our rejoicings were therefore sincere but measured. We had sneaking fears that we might soon find ourselves on the German front.

As it turned out, the battalion had reached its furthest point along the route, for we were to be ordered to move back on 9

November. We were proud to hear that the 11th Northumberland Fusiliers had been singled out for specific mention in Italian orders and this, coupled with our special mention for the June enemy offensive, constituted a quite special honour.

In the meantime all the usual steps were being taken to heal our wounds, and get the company back into working order. On the day following the armistice I was surprised to be called to company headquarters to be informed that I was being recommended for a stripe. I was genuinely annoyed, as I felt strongly that I ought now to see the war through as a private, a sort of inverted snobbery. I protested strongly, and was told curtly that my views were not being sought. The next day the stripe was sewn on to my sleeves by the company tailor and an awful conspicuousness settled about my arms. No one else seemed to be surprised. It may well be that my excessive modesty had been assessed as some sort of act. Of course I was in two minds about it all. In one sense, I had a sudden feeling of having lost my virtue, such absurd notions do we get when we are young. In another sense I was pleased with my new importance.

I was saved the normal course of holding unpaid rank for a period. Within twenty-four hours the promotion to the rank of paid lance-corporal was confirmed in battalion orders, and on the very morning, as luck would have it, the company paraded for section drill, an evolution that almost invariably ended in our getting thoroughly mixed up. In this, infrequently practised, drill the section leaders unusually had to issue commands. I was simply horrified at the prospect thus thrust upon me, doubtful as to the correct wording and startled to hear my own voice. Yet the section wheeled correctly and no one seemed to detect anything amiss. Instead of instilling confidence, the incident merely confirmed my feeling that it would have been better to leave things as they were at this late stage. I had no interest in relearning army drill from the NCO's point of view.

And so, on 9 November, the column was marching gaily back towards the Piave, singing with a new gusto all the old songs, songs that were to continue to ring down the ages, but regretting more than ever the gaps in our ranks, particularly that of our dead captain. I had been placed in charge of the company's Lewis gun limber, which brought up the rear with the gun swivelled in a firing position; for, despite the armistice, we were taking no chances. We had to keep to the minor roads, leaving the main routes clear for the supply columns. Crossing one of the small mountain streams we had a minor mishap, when the limber called for the attention of the farrier-sergeant. Otherwise the march was quite uneventful. On the second day we crossed the Piave by one of the new bridges. We could not help noticing that hereabouts the Austrian front-zone wire had been heavily shattered by our artillery barrage. If this had been done on our sector — situated a little further northwards — our casualties would most certainly have been lighter and some of our dead colleagues would have been present on this happier occasion. In all probability the neglect of the wire on our sector had been due to its proximity to the open flank, a slight error in mathematics at a spot which, in view of its importance and vulnerability, should have been given special attention by the gunners.

We were billeted for the night in a small village on the outskirts of Treviso, where I experienced for the first time some of the small worries of responsibility. Awakened in the small hours, I was deputed to take our ammunition supplies down to the dump. Not knowing the reason for this sudden emergency I had to employ all my persuasive powers, intermixed with slight threats of dire punishment, to get the members of my section out of their blankets. It was part of the system, and a tribute to the capacity of the lowest-ranking officer, that responsibility for fatigues of this sort were delegated right down the line to the lance-corporal, who even to his own men often figured as 'the onion'.

Getting out of the wrong side of the bed in this way was no indication that the grey dawn of 11 November promised anything but just another ordinary day. We left our billet early, but spent most of the day in an open field, waiting for someone to make up his mind. Towards evening we marched to the railway station, entrained once again for an unknown destination, and were served with supper. While we were still hanging about in the siding some passing Tommies told us quite casually that Germany also had given in. Despite our widely manifested scepticism we were filled with half suppressed excitement, hoping against hope that the impossible had really come to pass. As indeed it had. And it was thus that the shattering news came to us.

11: THE END?

Our night journey ended early in the morning at Tavernelle, whence we marched to billets in Arzignano; everyone was much too tired to bother about world events for the moment. However, by the evening, after a day of rumour, it was definitely confirmed that Germany had signed an armistice. Although a heavy weight had thus been lifted from all our hearts, there was little outward excitement. We had been sceptical about the Austrian halt and already there had been discussion of a move to the Tyrol. True, there had recently been optimistic reports in the papers about the turn of the tide in France, but such bursts of journalistic optimism had been a recurring symptom since the early end of the war had been confidently forecast way back in 1914, before it had really got started, and we could see no sufficient reason even now why the Germans should not make a stand in their own fatherland on the Rhine. We knew to our cost what fighters they were.

By 13 November the news really had sunk in. The armistice had begun at 11 o'clock on the morning of 11 November. This was victory. We had imagined that the whole world would rejoice, but out here in Italy we took it all quietly. There was a heartfelt sense of relief, too great for shouting, and a deep sadness that brought into our minds a sea of jostling faces of dead comrades. At the time we did not know of the delirious scenes that had taken place at home, especially in the cities, where the people had spontaneously staged a sort of national bacchanalia in the streets.

The decisiveness of the armistice terms, which were posted up on the boards, astounded us — long lists of heavy materials to be handed over, and special precautions to be taken. Only a defeated army could have agreed to so much. We were indeed convinced.

Our little town was soon in gala dress, with banners of welcome strung across the roads: 'A Thousand Thanks to our Allies', 'Welcome to the Blighty Boys'. The guard continued to mount at battalion headquarters, to the roll of drums and edification of the townsfolk. It would have been interesting to know what they really thought of it all. Not that we bothered much about this ceremonial. I could not help remembering the words I had heard with horror from the throats of blue-garbed wounded at Harrogate while I was there in training in the spring of 1916:

> *I want to go home, I want to go home*
> *I don't want to go to the trenches no more*
> *Where Jack Johnsons burst and whizz-bangs do roar*
> *Take me over the sea*
> *Where the Alleman cannot catch me*
> *Oh my, I don't want to die, I want to go home.*

Lugubrious doggerel indeed, but how close to the heartfelt truth of so many during all those agonising months.

Within a day or two it was announced that leave was to be restarted forthwith, and I knew that my name would be on the list. This filled me with an even greater excitement than the news of the armistice. I had been away for over eighteen months, and I doubt whether I could have stood the strain had I known at the outset it would be so long. Now those awful months of fear and anguish had passed, and sheer joy was bursting out of my soul. We, the fortunate ones, paraded at the orderly room on 17 November, fourteen in all from the battalion, and I was glad to see that my friend Doniger was one of the party. We were packed forty in each truck. As the weather had now turned very cold, with snow carpeting the plains as well as the mountains, we were not really unfortunate to be thus crowded together. There was even an overflow group occupying the brake compartment perched above the end of the truck, where they could hardly have been very warm.

Among our travelling companions was an artilleryman who had been with the British heavies supporting the Italians some months before Caporetto. Speaking as a gunner who had usually enjoyed reasonably comfortable quarters, he said that he had been frankly amazed at the way the infantryman had managed to stand the conditions in the line, particularly on the Western Front. He told us that things had been easy enough in Italy before our arrival. Only then had the war taken a new turn and they had begun to lose their privileges. At the time they had been on the point of receiving the Italian trench service medal, but to their great disappointment the idea had been dropped with the arrival of much larger British and French forces. We had heard about this and would ourselves have liked to wear the Italian decoration, to which we felt we were entitled, but our authorities had ruled against any such distinction being given to one army out of so many among the world-wide battle fronts.

It was not before 21 November that we reached Le Mans, where large bodies of American troops had been concentrated, and on the following day we embarked at Cherbourg on the *SS Prince George* for Southampton. All I remember of that crossing was my great relief at being able to stretch my legs at night after being cooped up for so long in the train, and the prodigality of having a large cheese left on deck for anyone to carve at with a bayonet. Such reckless rationing we had hardly ever known. My greatest joy the next morning, as the train steamed Londonwards, was to see the neat quilt of fields unravelling endlessly across the window. Surely there was not another countryside such as this in all the wide world? My heart was filled with such delight that even today I can recollect clearly those moments of heartfelt thankfulness. 'Breathes there the man with soul so dead, Who never to himself hath said, "This is my own, my native land!"' Today, I fear, a half century later, there are many that do.

At the end of fourteen crowded days I was again on the boat to Cherbourg. The leave had all been wonderful and none of us was reconciled to returning all the way to Italy, even for a short while, as we hoped it would be. Yet our picture of home had been considerably modified. We had known that things had been difficult, but had not fully realised the effects of shortages and high prices, of the impact of the heavy casualties at the front, and latterly of the ravages of influenza, which had been carrying off so many there. The ration books had surprised me, and also the use of saccharine tablets, which were universally served in place of sugar. On the other hand the reports of air raids seem to have been exaggerated, as we saw few signs of this kind of damage. After all we were hardened to that sort of thing. Among the people there now seemed to be a great urge to be gay. London was crowded with soldiers in uniform, mostly officers and bemedalled. The streets were gaily illuminated at night and all places of amusement were crowded. There seemed to be little realisation on the part of those that had stayed at home of what it had been like at the front. We who survived were obviously the lucky ones, but, while we were ready enough to admit this among ourselves, we did not like the others to infer as much. The diametrically opposed attitude of the two camps, which was to become apparent in the years following the war, was already emerging. One felt just a little chilled inside at the lack of understanding, for we considered that we deserved well of our countrymen. Already, although this was not to be borne upon us for some time, we were the members of a lost generation, and those who could have understood us best were no longer in this world.

Thus it was not an outstandingly happy party that halted at Le Mans on the evening of 9 December to enjoy a mess-tin of tea. Here there was talk of trouble between groups of Americans and Frenchmen, or 'Froggies' as they were disparagingly called. The natural, albeit good-natured, arrogance of the American did not please us very much, for we were too immediately aware that, as a nation, they had been standing on the sidelines while the rest of the Allies were sacrificing themselves in unmeasured slaughter.

The train halted again, for five hours this time, at St. Pierre des Corps, a little way past Tours. This was also an area of large American concentration camps (as they were called at the time). Two Yanks, heavily burdened with their packs, trudging alongside the railway, drew solicitous enquiries from the train. 'Where yer goin' Sam?' shouted a sympathetic voice. 'Up the line,' came the answer. A wag replied in mock disappointment. 'Too late, too late. It's all over.' The train rocked with laughter. During the wait an upstanding American sergeant strolled over for a chat. He had been in the trenches and knew all about the war, which, in fact, had not started until they came! They had, it seemed, improved upon everything we had. Even our rifles were antiquated; their sights all wrong, the bolt incapable of working quickly enough. We listened with simulated astonishment, and he went on talking. Unable to keep up pretence any longer many of us had to withdraw into the depths of the truck to stifle our mirth. But it was incredible, even though we knew well that our allies were quite sincere in their beliefs.

We got moving again. Travelling in this direction was much more comfortable than on the journey home. There were only 22 in our truck, and abundant supplies of fuel — coal, coke and wood. But rations were short and we had done well to lay in a good stock of eatables for the journey. On the third day we were creeping amidst the glories of the French Alps, with Mont Blanc ahead, but snow began to fall, obscuring the magnificent scene. It was 14 December before we detrained at Tavernelle and found the 11th Battalion comfortably billeted in the charming little township of Montecchia di Crosara set amidst pleasant hill country. Number 6 Platoon was occupying the stage of the village's delightful miniature theatre, while the rest of the company shared the auditorium. We were told that there had been high jinks on the company's arrival in this unusual billet, and the boys found the wardrobes and make-up boxes unlocked. The temptation had been too great to resist. After a crowd of weird characters had paraded the streets and nearly caused a riot, strict orders had been issued that the villagers' properties should be respected in the future. They were very naturally concerned about the fate of their excellently appointed theatre, with its scenery, properties and lighting equipment, and rightly so for it is doubtful whether any place in Britain could at that time have boasted anything so fine, and this was but an obscure townlet.

Everyone was now looking forward eagerly to demobilisation, active plans for which were being worked out. A new draft had joined us in the meantime, consisting partly of first-timers and partly of old campaigners who had recovered from wounds. They had crossed the Channel on the very eve of the armistice and would therefore all be entitled to the same general medals as the rest of us. It always seemed an anomaly and very unfair to me that the man who came for the first time on active service on the very last day of the war, should receive the same medals as the man who had crossed the waters as far back as 1 January 1916. Our senior NCOs had all been decorated for the last battle mainly as a matter of course since, in the absence of any officer survivors to make recommendations, the number of awards had been strictly limited. This is not to say that the awards were not generally well deserved, merely that they were unselective.

Everything was now being done to make parades as attractive as possible. The order had gone forth that the troops should be kept happy. There were even whist-drives. The projected school started — but much too belatedly — and classes in English, History, French, Arithmetic, Shorthand and Bookkeeping were available at a modest level. This was certainly an excellent development, but I was able to attend only the first history lecture, provided by the padre, before a purposeful job was found for me. This was to assist in the orderly room, a task for which I had no active desire at this stage. Like the rest I wanted to get out and feared that any definite assignment might delay the hoped-for moment. Sergeant-Major Rhodes, who had just returned to us after his wounding in the battle of 15 June, gave me a personal assurance that my acceptance would not delay my discharge when the time came.

I found plenty to do in the company office, the usual returns and routine duties being supplemented by the new work in connection with demobilisation. It was all very revealing to me. I suspect that the regular staff were getting a little out of their depth and were pleased to have a junior civil servant to help them. I did not really mind being occupied at all hours, as I now was, for there was little else to do. But I was less pleased at having to loosen contact with the platoon and transfer my blankets to the orderly room. It was this late-in-the-day opportunity to look behind the scenes that really startled me. I saw how the food of the staff, including the sergeants' and officers' messes, although nominally issued on the same basis as the rank and file, worked out so much better. This was to some extent due to the advantage of first choice — the best loaf, the least crumbly piece of cheese, the small item insufficiently large to divide among the entire company — and the more skilled and careful cooking. The war was over of course but rations were not generally in generous supply, and I deduced from the general attitudes in the orderly room that this is how more or less it had always been. I could now understand more clearly why runners and other specialist privates had always been keen on the company attachment, in spite of many obvious disadvantages. They were a privileged group. This impression was strongly reinforced the first time I had occasion to visit the officers' quarters, but this did not surprise me, for the situation was clearly known and apart from the accepted class distinctions of the time, which spread over to the holders of wartime commissions, there was the obvious point that those who had to plan and to lead needed to be relieved as much as possible from the hardships that the ranker was bound to endure. At this time at least the officers were very cosily accommodated, with normal middle-class amenities. It struck me at the time that their living room was indeed a home from home.

One of the first documents I saw among the official papers, contained brief citations for six names put forward to battalion headquarters for Military Medals in connection with the forthcoming New Years Honours list. I was surprised and not a little embarrassed to discover my name among them. Quite apart from the fact that I had never felt brave, or even capable of anything out of the ordinary on the battlefield, I was really shocked at the exaggerated terms in which all these recommendations were written. It is true that there had been hints from members of the platoon that something of this sort had been in the air, but I had taken it as nothing more than an ill-judged leg-pull and dismissed the whole matter from my mind. Now I was reading about myself and failing to recognise the image. It is true that the garbled facts appeared to relate to an incident during the last attack, but their lack of veracity made me blush not from pleasure but from shame. Yet the incident was illuminating as to the way such reports were dressed up. Nothing was to come of this as far as 'B' Company was concerned.

One day Doniger and I decided to grasp an opportunity to step outside our army life by obtaining a pass to the historic city of Verona. We were all up with the lark, seven members of the company, whose passes I had arranged. Our journey took us by bus, through Ronca and Montebello, to St. Bonifacio, where we changed into one of those steam trams that travelled alongside the road or across the fields. When approaching a halt on the outskirts of the city, which were as drab and uninteresting as any town suburbs could well be, an Italian soldier slipped from the connecting platform between the coaches to immediate death. It all happened in a flash. The irony of it: who knows what terrible risks the dead man had suffered during his service at the front, for his life to end so inconsequentially.

Such is the resilience of the human spirit, especially when confronted by the misfortunes of others, that we had forgotten the sad incident by the time we had left the terminus behind us and were walking into the town proper, at once entering streets of mediaeval shape and colour. Doniger and I, aided by a little paperback guidebook to Verona in English which we had found in a small general shop, were soon doing the place in proper tourist style, though certainly till then I had never enjoyed such an experience. We revelled in the unwonted freedom of the day, the friendliness we met at every turn from townsfolk who were so evidently amused at our open-hearted appreciation of their city, and above all we enjoyed seeing the many evidences of Verona's chequered history. There was the Duomo and the many fine churches, the charming cloisters of the Monastery of San Bernadino, the interesting ruins of the Roman theatre on the far bank of the river, the lovely Piazza d'Erbe, and in the adjoining courtyard, the tombs of the Scaligeri, one of Verona's celebrated families, still heavily shielded with sandbags against enemy bombing. Above all I was impressed by the vast and wonderfully constructed Roman Amphitheatre, with its tier upon tier of well-preserved stone seats, which we mounted to enjoy from the surrounding wall the fine panorama of the city and its hills. At the time the corridors and cavernous passages under the auditorium were stored with fuel, but in peacetime the vast arena had still been used for occasional entertainments and displays. Verona is largely contained within a double loop of the Adige, which is crossed by a number of picturesque bridges. The foothills, rising steeply on the northern bank, were studded with delightful white villas. In the afternoon sun, with the blue cloud-flecked sky above and the many towers of the town rising beyond the sparkling green waters, it seemed that I was gazing upon a city of dreams. I decided then that Italy was surely a land worth fighting for. Indeed, Verona, despite the shabby scars of war, was a place full of charm. I was to have the good fortune to visit it again within a year or two, and it was as lovely as ever, with its sidewalks now crowded with picturesque peacetime folk and its market stalls burdened with luscious fruits and lovely flowers. This was before modernisation and increasing motorisation was to crowd the beauty away into the alleyways. Fortunate indeed were those of an earlier generation who saw these places before the life spirit had been driven out by the machine.

Only once during that memorable day was life's dark side thrust under our notice. This was when, true to our chosen role, we entered a small shop to purchase some rather drab picture postcards as souvenirs. There a somewhat nondescript Italian soldier offered to take us to *le donne bellissime*, only to be thrust aside with disgust. Our last hour was spent in the Museo Civile, where we enjoyed the fine collection of objects representing the natural history and culture of the province. We were due back at the tram terminus at 4 pm, whither we made our way wondering how the rest of the party had got on, for throughout our peregrinations we had had fleeting glimpses of only two of them.

We quickly discovered that they had paid little attention to the city's historic attractions, but had found plenty to satisfy the demands of the flesh, which had been the sole reason for taking the trouble to travel thus far. As they retold their adventures noisily — for much recourse to *vino rosso* had greatly increased their volubility and romanticised their commercialised amours — and chipped us unmercifully for our guide-book camouflage, the whole tram rocked with laughter. Whether the good townsfolk, who were thus brought into the merriment, were aware that it all had to do with the seduction of their womenfolk, I can only guess.

Our Christmas day in 1918 was indeed an occasion for rejoicing, and the miniature theatre provided a wonderful setting for what was to be for many of us the last communal meal in the army. As a member of the company staff I spent the morning cutting sandwiches for the meal, which was fixed for 4 pm. With the band playing on the stage the meal was a great success: roast beef and roast pork; Christmas pudding and rum sauce; stewed fruit and custard; fresh fruits and rum punch in generous spate. It was a great occasion, though not much helped by the rather patchy extemporised concert that followed. The company was soon half tipsy and as usual the proceedings tended to degenerate into a brawl. The hefty company bully, whom I have mentioned and who was among those of us who had survived from the Ypres battles, happened to fall foul of a member of the recent draft, a lean old soldier, who was not prepared to permit liberties. I do not remember the bully having been taken at his word before, which is saying a lot in such a tough crowd that had always included its quota of good boxers. More than once had I been compelled to dig in my heels and hope for the best when a threatening stance was being taken near the food dixy, but nothing had ever come of it; which was as well for me. Now the challenge had been accepted without the slightest possibility of doubt. The contestants disappeared with a small following to the convenient vault under the stage, well masked by the racket going on above. The fight went furiously for a few moments, but was quickly over when a well-placed punch sprawled the bully to the ground, from which he rose a chastened man. It had been more or less as I had always suspected.

Work in the orderly room was increasing daily. We had to comb through the company to find two assistants to deal with the employment forms which each man had to submit, and there was a dearth of clerical talent available. Not only were the forms usually filled in so illegibly as to need rewriting, but we had the greatest difficulty in extracting the basic details of the man's previous employment, which were needed and often had to be dragged out of him by dint of persistent questioning. So much for our vaunted universal education.

Two drafts of miners, who were urgently wanted to get the pits in full production, were sent home without regard to length of service, and there was much murmuring in the ranks at the blatant unfairness of this policy, which again demonstrated how little the authorities understood the psychology of the men at the front. There was even more acute trouble in our sister battalion, and on the first day of 1919 the brigadier and commanding officer both addressed us, in an attempt to explain why this urgency had arisen. Had we but known it, this was a premonitionary example of the acts of communal unfairness by which our lives were destined to be dogged when we got back into civil life. Bureaucratic interpretations of the general need were rarely to coincide with what to us were the norms of individual justice.

On 4 January we left Montecchia di Crosara, with much regret, for it had been a very pleasant stopping place, and marched twenty-eight kilometres, through Monteforte, Sambonifacio and San Stefano, along execrable roads, to Zimella, a much less attractive spot, though our billets were comfortable enough. On the following day my promotion to the rank of full corporal came through battalion orders.

Another draft of miners left, many of whom had been abroad only a couple of months, and few more than six months. Everyone was fed up and unrest was becoming widespread. This sparked off trouble with Allied troops in many areas. Then we were buoyed up with the news that general demobilisation was about to start. The troops were lectured on the advantages of re-enlistment for short terms of service, with the prospects of a good bounty at the end, but the response could hardly have encouraged the authorities.

One afternoon I was called upon to give evidence before a court of enquiry regarding a senior member of the company who had gone on leave at the same time as myself and had not returned. He had been a first-rate soldier with many medal awards to his credit, but his impatience with the purposeless army life now that fighting had ceased had thus led to his trial *in absentia* for desertion, though I doubt whether steps were subsequently taken to carry out the findings of the court. There must have been too many others in similar circumstance.

On the day when the sergeant, who was acting as CQMS, went into Verona, I was left in full charge of the orderly room, and I had cause to ponder over the rapidity with which new responsibilities were piling upon me. On this occasion I was astonished at the number of returns and other routine tasks that had to be completed on one such day as this. One case I handled concerned one of our cooks, who had to be bundled off to hospital for treatment for venereal disease. He was an old hand who had worked in the cookhouse for some time. I remembered him because subsequently I noticed his name in one of the minor awards list, MSM I think it was.

But my time was running short. It was a neck-and-neck race between mounting responsibilities and my turn for demobilisation. On 17 January my 'release slip' arrived from England. This was the essential document signed by the soldier's employers — the Post Office Stores Department in my case — certifying that his job was open for him. Two days later the acting CQMS went on leave and I found myself in complete charge. It looked as though my release would be delayed. The new Company Commander proposed to veto it, but Sergeant-Major Rhodes, who had given his word, spoke up strongly on my behalf and my name was put on the next departure list.

Looking back over the years I find it difficult to understand why I was not prepared to wait just a little longer to help the battalion. There were even prospects of an early trip to Venice, which I had been arranging with Doniger, but the magnet of home was too powerful. It had been so long; the dispatch of miners out of turn had made us all fed up with the army authorities. Furthermore, the death of so many of our officers and now the continuing disappearance of so many close colleagues had reduced almost to nothing any loyalty we may have had for the unit, in which we had certainly come to take a great deal of pride. Despite the love we had for some of our companions, to many of us army life had always been a sort of penance. To go home was to go back into the world of freedom, and who would stay in prison for an additional few hours if it could be avoided? We should all have liked to march home together, but the battalion was virtually dissolving before our eyes. It was the hour of anti-climax.

I received my papers, including a formal certificate of good conduct, from the demobilisation officer on 24 January, took leave of Doniger, who was to stay on for a while and to accompany the force assigned for garrison duty in Austria, and on the following day I boarded the train for the long journey home. It was to take nearly seven days, but nobody minded. Each man had three blankets and a leather jerkin, which we felt would amply keep us warm. As we marched to the siding the sun shone brilliantly upon the panorama of plain and snow-clad mountain with which Italy was to dismiss her erstwhile saviours. Only temporarily in my case, I am glad to say, for I was frequently to find occasion to come back and indeed to widen my knowledge of that lovely land.

Two incidents on the journey call for brief mention, as indicative of the unchanging essence of human nature. The first was at Voghera, where the train halted to allow us to wash. A trainload of Germans in course of repatriation was drawn up in the siding — officers, rankers, nurses — some dressed in correct Prussian style and even behaving in the arrogant way so tellingly caricatured in the magazines of the times. One of them, who could speak English, came over and told us how fed up they had been with the never-ending war. But when asked whether they would ever fight again, with a queer look they replied that their children might. I must confess I did not find this funny, and an angry shudder ran down my spine. That was a look I was not to forget. The second incident happened at Paray-le-Monail two days later when we stopped for tea. There was a troop train on another line, with soldiers from Egypt, which, we were told, was being searched. Our dawdling through the previous night was accounted for. It was said that at a halt further back a French girl had been sexually assaulted by a party of men from the train. It happened that she was the mayor's daughter and the matter was being taken seriously.

We crossed the Channel on the last day of January in the *USS Napotin*, and I reached the dispersal camp on Wimbledon Common at 8 pm to sit down at once to a hot meal. For some unexplained reason our discharge was not to begin before 1 am the following morning, and for the last time the army was to make us wait.

The last roll was called at 12.30 am on 1 February 1919, and the process of divesting us of our army personalities and

266

responsibilities, which was to be completed at 4 am, proceeded through the following measured, carefully organised, stages:

Stage 1: Rifles inspected for live ammunition. Papers checked.

Stage 2: Equipments stripped down and packed in valise. Sandbag issued to carry away small kit, which we were to keep.

Stage 3: Particulars taken for clothes. We retained our khaki uniform and steel helmets. In addition we were offered a civil suit and overcoat, or an allowance in lieu. In view of the army made-to-pattern look of the clothing I chose the allowance, insufficient as it was to prove in the shops.

Stage 4: Out-of-work Donation Book issued. This I did not need as a civil servant, but it was to provide many who were without work with a weekly payment from the Employment Exchange, without having to qualify for Unemployment Insurance Benefit.

Stage 5: An Identity Certificate issued — this I was to have stolen during the next few months.

Stage 6: Surrendered Pay Book at the Pay Office and received a cash advance of £2, on account of the Bounty which was due to be paid to each of us, varying according to rank.

Stage 7: Papers finally checked and completed.

Stage 8: Railway warrants checked (not required in my case as I lived on the doorstep) and demobilisation completed.

I spent the rest of the night before the YMCA fire, awaiting the morning light. It is not the experience of many in this life to be reborn, but that is how I felt on that early 1919 day when I was well into my twenty-second year. It was all over. A nightmare had been lifted from my soul. I still remember the bright morning, as I left the temporary camp on the common and walked, with a spring even in my heavy army boots, down Putney Hill back into civil life. It was indeed a new day on which one's heart was loaded down with gratitude to God for being allowed to live when so many worthier men had laid down their lives, or been maimed. I was even so presumptuous as to glory in my service and to feel that, despite my personal weaknesses, I had not betrayed the trust that had been placed on my shoulders.

It was indeed a new day, and I knew how pleased my mother would be at my final return. Of course, I did not realise it then — and it is doubtful whether any realised it — that the new day was at the beginning of a new world, in which we would have to say goodbye to 'all our yesterdays'. A time would come when many of us would regret the world that had passed, some would even struggle hopelessly to have it reinstated, but to no avail. For better or for worse we were dedicated to the future. In a bare twenty years those who had survived the intervening ordeals of the peace would finally face the certitude that 'for worse' it had been.

A NOTE TO THE READER

If you have enjoyed this book enough to leave a review on **Amazon** and **Goodreads**, then we would be truly grateful.
The Estate of Norman Gladden

Sapere Books is an exciting new publisher of brilliant fiction and popular history.

To find out more about our latest releases and our monthly bargain books visit our website:
saperebooks.com

Printed in Dunstable, United Kingdom

71158321R00157